TEM

MW00460228

RESISTED AND REPULSED

THE TREASURES OF JOHN OWEN

TEMPTATION

RESISTED AND REPULSED

Abridged and made easy to read by
Richard Rushing

THE BANNER OF TRUTH TRUST

THE BANNER OF TRUTH TRUST

Head Office
3 Murrayfield Road
Edinburgh
EH12 6EL
UK

North America Sales
PO Box 621
Carlisle
PA 17013
USA

banneroftruth.org

Originally published in 1658
This edition first published 2007
© Richard Rushing 2007

Reprinted 2012
Reprinted 2018

*

ISBN
Print: 978 0 85151 947 0

*

Typeset in 10.5/14 Sabon Oldstyle
at The Banner of Truth Trust, Edinburgh

Printed in the USA by
Versa Press Inc.,
East Peoria, IL.

Contents

Author's Preface

CHRISTIAN READER,

If you are at all awake in these days in which we live, and have taken notice of the manifold, great, and various temptations which beset all sorts of persons that know the Lord and profess his name, and to which they are continually exposed, and what success these temptations have obtained, to the unspeakable scandal of the gospel, and the wounding and ruin of innumerable souls, you will need no further reason for the publishing of these warnings and directions suited to the times that are passing over us and to your own concern in them.

But my bringing these meditations to public view arose first from the encouragement of friends with an interest in advancing Christ's cause in the world by personal holiness and by adhering to things precious to him. This gives them a powerful influence over me to accomplish things of such importance. This is not to say, of course, that I did not myself feel how seasonable and necessary the work was. The variety of outward providences I have experienced in the world and the inward trials that have, attended them, along with the observations I have been able to make of the ways and walk of others, their beginnings, progress, and endings, their risings and fallings, in profession and conversation, in darkness and light, all these have left such a constant sense and impression on my mind and spirit of the power and danger of temptation that, even with no other reason, I cannot but own a serious call to men to beware to be very necessary, and seek to show them some of the main ways in which, in my own judgment, temptations are prevailing at present.

But now, reader, if you are among those who take no notice of these things and care nothing for them, having no sense of the efficacy and danger of temptation in your own walk and profession, not observing its power over others, not seeing the great advantage temptation has obtained in these days in which everything is being shaken, not troubled or moved by the sad success temptation has achieved over professors, supposing that all is well, but thinking things would be better if you could only obtain a fuller satisfaction of some of your lusts in the pleasures and profits of the world: I want to tell you that I am not writing for you, nor do I think you a competent judge of what I have written.

At a time when all the issues of providence with respect to the public affairs of these nations[1] are confused, the footsteps of God being in the deep, and his paths not known (see *Psa.* 77:19); when unparalleled distresses and

---

[1] Owen means the nations of the British Isles. He was writing in 1658, the year of Oliver Cromwell's death.

strange prosperities are measured out to men, even to professors; when a spirit of error, folly, and delusion goes forth with such strength and power that it seems to have received a commission to go and prosper (see 1 *Kings* 22:12–15); and when there is so much division, strife, and rivalry, together with such evil imaginations, wrath, and revenge among brethren; when the desperate outcomes of men's temptations are seen daily in partial and total apostasy, the decay of love, the overthrow of faith, our days being filled with such fearful examples of backsliding as former ages never knew; when there is a visible decline from reformation seen among the professing Christians of these nations, both in personal holiness and in zeal for Christ: anyone who does not perceive that there is an 'hour of temptation' come upon the world, to try those who dwell upon the earth (see *Rev.* 3:10), must either be himself taken captive by the power of some woeful lust, corruption, or temptation, or is indeed utterly blind, not knowing at all what it is to serve God in temptations. To such I do not propose at present to speak.

As for those who have a sense of these things, and see that the plague has begun (see *Num.* 16:46–47), this warning is intended for them, so that they may be further awakened to look about them, in case the infection has come nearer to them, by some secret and imperceptible ways, than they had realized; and in case they should be taken unawares by the temptations that waste at noon, or walk in darkness (see *Psa.* 91:6). What I say is meant for those who mourn in secret for all the abominations found among those who profess the gospel, and for those who, under the guidance of the Captain of their salvation, are fighting and resisting the power of temptations, whatever their source.

That our faithful and merciful High Priest, who has both suffered and been tempted, and is therefore touched by the feeling of our infirmities, would accompany this small discourse with seasonable supplies of his Spirit, and suitable mercy to those who shall consider it, so that it may be useful to his servants for the ends intended, is the prayer of him who received this handful of seed from Christ's storehouse and treasure,

JOHN OWEN
Oxford, 1658

I

Introduction

Watch and pray, that ye enter not into temptation
(Matt. 26:41)

These words of our Saviour are repeated with very little alteration by the three Evangelists. Matthew and Mark record them as above. Luke says 'Rise and pray, lest you enter into temptation'; the whole caution seems to have been, 'Arise, watch and pray, that you enter not into temptation.'

Solomon tells us of some that lie down on the top of a mast or in the midst of the sea (*Prov.* 23:34). This is an accurate picture of men who are overtaken by a false security at the brink of destruction. If any have ever done so, the disciples in the garden certainly did! Their Master was just a little distance from them offering up prayer and supplications, with strong crying and tears (*Heb.* 5:7), while they slept. He was beginning to taste the cup that was filled with the curse and wrath due to their sins. The Jews were nearby and armed for *his* and *their* destruction!

Jesus had earlier informed them that this was the night of his coming betrayal and death. The disciples saw that Jesus was sorrowful, and very heavy (*Matt.* 26:37). He had even told them plainly that his soul was 'exceeding sorrowful, even unto death' (verse 38), and he entreated them to wait and watch with him. He was dying, and dying for them! In this condition, as he left them for a little while, like men who had forsaken all their love toward him or care for themselves, they fell fast asleep! Even the best of saints, being left to themselves will quickly appear to be less than men, to be nothing.

All of our own strength is weakness, and all of our own wisdom is folly. Peter was one of those that fell asleep, and that soon after he had expressed such self-confidence that he would not forsake him even if all others did! Our Saviour said to Peter; 'Could you not watch with me for one hour?' It seems to be implied in his words that if Peter could not watch just one hour, he was not likely to fulfil his boast never to forsake him! As if to say, 'Could you really hold out, if you cannot even watch with me for an hour? Is this how you are going to die for me, being dead in security while I am dying for you?'

It is an amazing thing to consider that Peter should make so high a promise, and then immediately be so careless and remiss in the pursuit of it.

We find however in our own hearts the same root of treachery abiding and working. It bears fruit in us every day, the most noble promises of obedience quickly ending in deplorable negligence (*Rom.* 7:18).

The Lord Jesus sought to stir them up to see their condition, their weakness, their danger. Ruin lay right at the door! They needed to rise, watch, and pray.

In this study we will not be considering the specific testing that Christ had in mind which was about to fall upon these disciples in the scandal and events of the cross. My purpose is to consider in these words a general principle that applies to all of Christ's disciples throughout all generations. There are three things in Christ's words:

1. The *evil* cautioned against — *temptation.*
2. The *means* by which it prevails — by our *entering into it.*
3. The *way* of preventing it — *watch* and *pray.*

The word for temptation is used in two ways in the New Testament: (1) In general, to test, or prove. Thus God is said to test, and we are commanded as our duty to test, try, or search ourselves to know what is in us, and to pray that God would also do so. Affliction tests us, and James exhorts that we count it all joy when we meet trials (*James* 1:2). In Genesis 22:1, we see God testing Abraham. (2) Secondly, testing in the negative sense is to seek to lead the soul into evil. We generally translate it temptation. In this sense, God tempts no one, and Christ exhorts us to pray that we do not enter into temptation.

Thus temptation is like a knife. It may be useful to cut the meat, or to cut the throat of a man. It may be a man's food or his poison, his exercise or his destruction.

It is not my intention to go deeply into the general nature of testing, as seen in the trials mentioned above, but to consider the danger of temptation to sin, and the means of preventing that danger. For clarity, however, I will consider as a preface something of the nature of testing in general, as seen in the trials of the saints.

2

The General Nature of Testing

As to the testing of ourselves by God, we will consider two things: 1. The reasons for which he does it, and 2. The way in which he does it.

1. The reasons for which God tests us.

First, he does it *to show man what is in his heart.* He would have us see either the grace or corruption that dwells there. (I am not now speaking of the place that testing may have in judicial hardening.) Grace and corruption lie deep in the heart, and man is often deceived in his evaluations of it. God comes to us with a gauge that can go right to the bottom. His instruments of trial dig right into the depths and innermost parts of the soul. This allows man to see clearly what is truly in him, and what type of metal is in his constitution. God tested Abraham to show him his faith. Abraham did not know what power and vigour was in his faith until God drew it out by that great trial and testing (*Gen.* 22:1–2). God tried

Hezekiah to discover his pride; he left him that he might see what was in his heart (2 *Chron.* 32:31). Hezekiah did not know he had such a proud heart, or one so prone to be lifted up in boasting, until he was tested. The testing revealed all the filth and poured it out before him. Trials can also reveal our thankfulness, our humility, etc. which we will not now consider.

Secondly, God allows man to be tested *to show himself to man*. Until we are tested, we think that we are living on our own strength. It is however, God alone who keeps us from falling by his *preventing grace*. We might say, 'All men may do this or that, but *we* will not!' When the trial comes, however, we quickly see that only God's preservation upholds us. So it was with Abimelech (*Gen.* 20:6), God withheld him from sinning. God also reveals his *renewing grace* through our testings. Paul, in his prayer for deliverance from his thorn in the flesh, found God's sufficiency and renewing grace (2 *Cor.* 12:9). We do not realize the power and strength that God puts forth on our behalf, and the sufficiency of his grace, until we compare our trials with our weakness. God's power and grace are then seen clearly in our lives. The effectiveness of an antidote is not realized until one has been exposed to the poison. The preciousness of a medicine is revealed by the presence of the disease. We will not know the power of grace until we feel the power of the testing. We must be tried, to realize the glory of being preserved. There are many other gracious ends that God has to accomplish in his saints by their trials which we will not consider now.

2. *Some of the ways that God accomplishes this.*

First: God sets men *great tasks* that are beyond their strength to accomplish. So he tested Abraham in the duty of sacrificing his son. It was a thing absurd to reason, bitter to nature, and grievous to him on all accounts whatsoever. Many men do not know what is in them, or rather what is available to them, until they are asked to do something utterly beyond their strength. The duties that God has for us along our ordinary path of life are not in proportion to the strength we have in ourselves, but in proportion to the help and relief that is laid up for us in Christ. By God's strength we are able to perform the most difficult tasks even though we only have the ability for the small ones. This is the law of grace. Few realize this important truth. Difficult and extraordinary duties appear before us as trials in our union with Christ, but his strength is able to overcome all.

Second: A second way that God accomplishes this is by putting his people through *great sufferings*. How many have unexpectedly found strength to die at a stake, or to endure tortures for Christ! Victory comes by his grace, though at first it seems like a great trial. Peter reveals how we are tested (*1 Pet.* 1:6–7). Our testing arrives as we pass through 'fiery trials', which come for the testing of our faith.

3

What Is Temptation?

God in his providence allows occasions of temptation to be administered to men, such as the case of false prophets mentioned in Deuteronomy 13:3. They are not however temptations from God. They do not come from him, and therefore they are different from our previous considerations. This brings us to the main purpose of our study, the consideration of these temptations which do not come from God, and which have as their active purpose to lead us into sin. In this case, temptation may proceed either from Satan alone, from the world, from other men in the world, or from ourselves. Temptation may come from each of these individually, or they may join forces in various combinations.

1. *Satan tempts sometimes by himself* without taking advantage from the world, the things and persons in it, or ourselves. He seeks to inject his evil and blasphemous thoughts about God into the hearts of the saints. It is his own work. He does not use the world or our own hearts

in this temptation. No one would conceive of God and think evil of him. Satan is alone in this sin, and shall be so in the punishment. These fiery darts are prepared in the forge of his own malice, and shall, with all their venom and poison, be returned into his own heart for ever.

2. *Sometimes Satan makes use of the world*, and joins forces against us, without any help from within our hearts. This is the way he tempted our Saviour, by showing Him all the kingdoms of the world, and the glory of them (*Matt.* 4:8). The variety of assistants that Satan will use from the world to tempt us comprises all sorts and an innumerable number of instruments and weapons.

3. At other times, *Satan seeks assistance from ourselves*. We are not like Christ when Satan came to tempt him. Jesus declared that Satan had nothing in him (*John* 14:30). It is otherwise with us. Satan has in us an agreeable party within our very own breasts, for most of his ends (*James* 1:14, 15). This is how he tempted Judas. He appealed to the lust of Judas himself as he planted in his heart the idea of betraying Christ; he entered into him (*Luke* 22:3). Satan set the things of the *world* at work in Judas in providing thirty pieces of silver. He used the priests and the Pharisees as instruments, and appealed to Judas' own corruption, for he was covetous, a thief, and had the bag (*John* 12:6).

I might show how the world and our own corruptions act independently by themselves, and sometimes in conjunction with Satan and one another in this business of temptation. But the truth is that the ways and means of temptations, the kinds, degrees, and efficacy of them, and the causes of them, are so inexpressibly large and various, and the circumstances of them, from providence, nature, conditions spiritual and natural, with particular cases arising, are so innumerable, that it is impossible to organize them in a systematic way. To attempt it would be an endless task. I shall be satisfied to give a description of the general nature of that of which we must beware. This will suffice to accomplish the goal I have set myself.

A temptation, then, in general is *anything that, for any reason, exerts a force or influence to seduce and draw the mind and heart of man from the obedience which God requires of him to any kind of sin.*

In particular, it is a temptation if it causes a man to sin, gives him opportunity to do so, or causes him to neglect his duty. Temptation may suggest evil to the heart, or draw out the evil that is already there. It is also a temptation to a man if something is by any means able to distract him from his communion with God, or the consistent universal obedience that is required of him.

To clarify, I am considering temptation not just as the active force of seduction to sin, but also the thing itself by which we are tempted. Whatever it is, within us or without us, that hinders us from duty or provides an occasion for sin, this should be considered temptation. It could be business, employment, the course of one's life, company, affections, nature, corrupt purposes, relations, delights, honour, reputation, esteem, position, abilities, gifts, etc., that provide the opportunity to sin or neglect duty. These are true temptations just as much as the most violent solicitations of Satan or allurements of the world. Whoever does not realize this is on the brink of ruin.

4

Entering into Temptation

Entering into temptation is not merely being tempted. We will never be free from temptation while Satan continues in his power and malice, and while the world and lust continue. There is no promise in Scripture that we shall not be tempted at all. There is no occasion to pray for an absolute freedom from temptation, since there is no scriptural promise to claim concerning it. The direction that we do have is, 'Lead us not into temptation' (*Matt.* 6:13). It is *entering into temptation* that we are to pray against.

It is possible to be tempted, yet not enter into temptation. More is intended by the expression, 'Lead us not into temptation', than the ordinary work of Satan and our own lusts which will be sure to tempt us every day. There is something specific in entering into temptation that is not the saints' everyday work. It is something that befalls them particularly in reference to sin's seduction on one account or another. It is an entrance into a powerful or frightening allurement.

Entering into temptation does not mean that you have been conquered by it. It does not mean that you commit the sin or evil. A man may 'enter into temptation' and yet not fall under temptation. God can make a way of escape. When a man has entered into temptation God can break the snare, tread down Satan, and make the soul more than a conqueror. Christ entered into temptation, but was not in the least foiled by it!

The apostle calls it to 'fall into temptation' (*1 Tim.* 6:9), as a man falls into a pit or deep place where there are traps and snares with which he might be entangled. The man is not instantly killed or destroyed, but he is entangled and detained. He does not know how to get free or be at liberty. So Paul speaks in 1 Corinthians 10:13 in terms of temptation *taking* us. To be 'taken' by a temptation is to be tangled with it, to be held in its cords, and not find at present a way to escape. Peter also says in 2 Peter 2:9, 'The Lord knoweth how to deliver the godly out of temptations.' If they are entangled with them, God knows how to deliver them out of them. When we allow a temptation to enter into us, then we 'enter into temptation'. When sin knocks at the door, we are at liberty; but when a temptation comes in and we allow it to speak with our heart, reason with our mind, entice and allure our affections, for a long or short time, then sin subtly and almost imperceptibly draws our soul to take particular notice of it: we 'enter into temptation'.

For us to enter into temptation there must be two things: *First*, by some special advantage or occasion,

Satan attacks us with greater force than his ordinary solicitations to sin. He uses fears, allurements, persecutions, seductions, by himself or by others. He takes advantage of a lust or corruption and by his instigation it approaches us to provoke us or terrify us with a much greater disturbance than usual. When we enter into temptation there has been special activity of Satan to take particular advantage of us. *Secondly,* Our heart must be entangled enough in the temptation to cause it to rise up in its own defence, yet not to be wholly able to eject or cast out the poison or leaven that has been injected. The soul is surprised how hard to resist the entanglement is, since it has only slightly slipped from its faithfulness. The soul may cry, pray, and cry again, and yet not be delivered; as Paul 'besought the Lord' three times for the departure of his temptation, yet with no success. The entanglement continues.

Entering into temptation occurs in one of two seasons:

1. When God allows Satan, for ends best known to himself, to gain a peculiar advantage against the soul, as in the case of Peter: he sought to sift him like wheat, and prevailed.

2. When a man's lusts and corruptions meet a particularly provoking object or opportunity along life's way, as it was with King David. When one enters into one of these seasons, he has entered into temptation. Scripture calls it 'the hour of temptation' (*Rev.* 3:10). The hour of temptation is the hour that a temptation has arrived at its zenith. This helps us to understand the nature of entering

into temptation. When the hour of temptation has come upon us, we have entered into temptation. Every great and pressing temptation has its hour, a season in which it grows to its greatest force, when it is most vigorous, active, operative, and prevalent. It may take a while to get to this point, but given the right circumstances, outward or inward, temptation arrives at this very dangerous hour.

When temptation has arrived at its hour, a man has entered into it. The outcome is that the temptation has power over a man and carries him quite away before it, when at other times it has little or no power over him. Then he can despise it, laugh at its expression, and easily resist it. But temptation at times is supported by other circumstances and occurrences that give it new strength and effectiveness. The man is weakened; the hour has come, he has entered into it, and it prevails. David in his younger days had probably had temptations to commit adultery or murder, as in the case of Nabal, but the hour of temptation had not come, it did not have a strong advantage, and he escaped. Those who are exposed to temptation should look out, and who is not tempted?

All will experience a season in which their temptations will be more urgent, sin's reasonings more plausible, its pretensions more glorious, hopes of recovery seemingly clearer, opportunities broader and more open, the doors of evil more beautiful than ever they have been before. Blessed is he who is prepared for such a season! There is no escape without this preparation. If we maintain our preparation, we are safe.

5

Temptation's Hour

Before we turn to particulars, let us consider:

1. How or by what means a temptation commonly attains its hour.
2. How we may know when any temptation has come to its high noon, and is in its hour.
3. The means of the prevention prescribed by our Saviour.

1. *Temptation obtains its hour in three ways:*

i. *By long solicitations*, causing the mind frequently to converse with the evil temptation. Frequent temptations promote further thoughts about the evil. If temptation can accomplish this, it is approaching its hour. It may be that when the temptation first began to press upon the soul, the soul was amazed with the ugly appearance of what it aimed at, and cried, 'Am I a dog?' Even if the temptation is not daily heightened the soul, by conversing with the evil, begins to become, as it were, familiar with it, and is not so startled by it as formerly.

Familiarity tends to cause the heart to say, 'Is it not a little one?' When the heart says that, temptation is approaching its high noon. At that point lust has been enticed and entangled, and is ready to conceive (*James* 1:15).

ii. *By prevailing over others* in such a way that the soul is not filled with dislike and abhorrence of them and their ways, nor with pity and prayer for their deliverance. When sin has prevailed against others it increases its advantage also against us. The failure of Hymenæus and Philetus is said to 'overthrow the faith of some' *(2 Tim. 2:17–18)*.

iii. *By intermingling itself with other considerations that perhaps are not absolutely evil.* The Galatians' fall from the purity of the gospel might have been mixed with freedom from persecution, and union and consent with the Jews. Things good in themselves were included in the temptation.

2. *How we can recognize when a temptation has come to its hour.*

i. A temptation has come to its hour when it is *restless, urgent, and argumentative*. It is a time of battle, and sin will give the soul no rest. Satan sees his advantage, the convergence of his forces, and knows that he must now prevail, or be hopeless forever. Satan pushes this opportunity and time of advantage with special pleas and promises. He has taken some ground in his arguments so far, and seeks to extend his ground further. He reminds you of a full pardon after the sin. He realizes that if he does not win now, he will lose the opportunity. When Satan had prepared everything against Christ, it was the hour of darkness. With us, when a temptation presses in upon us through our imagination and reason, and when opportunities, solicitations, and advantages press us from outside, let your soul know that the hour of temptation's power has come. The glory of God depends upon victory in this trial.

ii. A temptation has also come to its hour when it *brings both fear and allurements together* to work with greater force. These came together in King David when he planned the murder of Uriah. There was the fear of retribution for his sin with Bathsheba, and the fear of his sin being found out. There was also the continued pleasure and enjoyment of her whom he lusted after. Men sometimes are carried into sin just by the love of it, but they often persist and remain in it because of the fear of the consequences that might follow repentance and full disclosure. When our reasonings run between our lust and our fear, and are ready to entangle us, we know it is the hour of temptation.

3. *Our Saviour teaches us how to avoid entering into temptation: 'Watch', and 'Pray'.*

The first of these is a general expression that means more than just being awake. *To watch* means to be on guard, to take heed, and to consider all the ways and means that the enemy might use to approach us; so Paul urges the Corinthians (*1 Cor.* 16:13) to be watchful, to stand firm in the faith, to act like men, and to be strong. We are to take heed and be careful; as we also read in Revelation 3:2, 'Be watchful, and strengthen the things that remain, that are ready to die: for I have not found thy works perfect before God.' Everyone needs to pay close attention to the ways and means provided by God to keep our hearts from getting entangled in the allurements and subtleties of Satan, and the occasions and advantages of sin in the world.

The second direction is *to pray*. This important duty is known to all. These two duties are the whole endeavour of faith to preserve us from temptation.

6

Our Great Duty:
To Avoid Temptation

Having laid the groundwork of the truth to be addressed and improved, I will now make this observation:

> *It is the great duty of all believers to use all diligence in the ways Christ has appointed, so as not to fall into temptation.*

I know God is 'able to deliver the godly out of temptations'. I know also, that he is 'faithful' and will not 'suffer us to be tempted above that we are able', but will 'make a way to escape'. I shall seek, however, to convince all who will pay attention to what I say that it is our great duty and concern to use all diligence, watchfulness, and care that we enter not into temptation; and I shall prove this by the following considerations:

1. In the ample *instructions given us by our Saviour concerning what we should pray for, this matter of not*

entering into temptation is prominent. Our Saviour knew how important it was for us to not enter into temptation, in that he gave it as a special topic in our daily dealing with God, 'Lead us not into temptation, but deliver us from evil' (*Matt.* 6:13). The order of the words also shows us how important it is. If we are first led into temptation, evil will befall us more or less. Christ's purpose for us is to seek his help in our daily prayers that we may be powerfully delivered from that evil which attends every entry into temptation.

Our blessed Saviour knows full well our state and condition. He knows the power of temptations, having experienced it (*Heb.* 2:18). He also knows our vain confidence in our ability to deal with temptations, as he found in Peter. He knows our weakness and folly, and how soon we are cast to the ground. That is why he has provided this important instruction. We greatly need to be aware how important this instruction is to us. If we trust the wisdom, love, and care of Christ Jesus toward us, we must accept the importance of this instruction.

2. Christ promises freedom and deliverance from temptation as a great *reward for obedience* (*Rev.* 3:10). This is the great promise made to the church of Philadelphia, in which Christ found nothing to blame, that they would be kept from the hour of temptation. Note that Christ did not say that he would keep them *through* temptation, but *from* it! 'There is', said our Saviour, in effect, 'an hour of temptation coming; a season that will make havoc in the

world. Multitudes shall fall from the faith, and deny and blaspheme me. Oh, how few will be able to stand and hold out! Some will be utterly destroyed, and perish forever. Others will get wounds to their souls that shall never be thoroughly healed while they live in this world. They will have their bones broken, and limp all their days!' Christ promises, however, that because some have kept the word of his patience, he will be tender towards them and keep them from this hour of temptation. Certainly that which Christ has promised to his beloved church, as a reward for her service, love, and obedience, is no light thing. Whatever Christ has promised to his spouse is the fruit of unspeakable love. This is just what is promised as a reward for special obedience.

3. Consider some *consequences of falling into temptation*, in the case of both bad and good men, ungrounded professors and the choicest of saints.

First, as to *ungrounded professors,* consider Luke 8:13: 'They on the rock are they, which, when they hear, receive the word with joy, and have no root, but for a while believe.' Well! How long do they believe? They are affected with the preaching of the Word, believe in it, make a profession, bring forth some fruits, but until what point do they abide? – 'In the time of temptation they fall away.' When once they enter into temptation, they are gone forever! Temptation withers all their profession, and slays their souls. We see this happening every day. Men have heard the preaching of the gospel, have been affected and delighted with it, have made a profession of it, and have been looked on, it may be, as believers, and thus have continued for some years, and yet no sooner does vigorous and continued temptation befall them than they turn out of the way, and are gone for ever. They come to hate the Word they once delighted in. They despise the professors of it, and are hardened by sin. So Matthew 7:26: 'He that hears these sayings of mine, and doeth them not, is like unto a foolish man, which built his house upon the sand.' What does this house of profession do for a man? It shelters him, keeps him warm, and stands for a while. But note verse 27: When the rain descends, when temptation comes, it falls utterly, and its fall is great.

Judas followed our Saviour three years, and all went well with him. Then as soon as he entered into temptation, Satan got him, and winnowed him, and he was gone! Demas preached the gospel until the love of the world fell on him, and he utterly turned aside. It would be an endless task to give instances. Entering into temptation, with this sort of men, is surely an entrance into apostasy, more or less, in part or in whole.

Secondly, consider the outcome of entering into temptation for *the saints of God* themselves.

Adam was the 'son of God' (*Luke* 3:38), created in the image of God, full of that integrity, righteousness, and holiness which were eminently like the holiness of God. He had a far greater inherent stock of ability than we, and he had nothing in him to entice or seduce him. But as soon as Adam entered into temptation he was gone, lost,

[23]

and ruined, he and all his posterity with him! What can we expect, if we also enter into temptation? We, like him, have the temptation and the cunning of the devil to deal with, but we also have a cursed world and a corrupt heart to increase the power of temptation.

Abraham was the father of the faithful, set forth as an example for all believers to follow. Yet he, entering twice into the same temptation, fear about his wife, was twice overpowered by it, to the dishonour of God, and no doubt to the disturbance of his own soul (*Gen.* 12:12–13; 20:2).

David is called a man after God's own heart, by God himself (*1 Sam.* 13:14), yet what a dreadful thing is the story of his entering into temptation! He was no sooner entangled but he was plunged into adultery. He then sought deliverance by his own invention, and like a poor creature in a net, he was entangled more and more until he lay down as one dead under the power of sin and folly.

I might mention *Noah, Lot, Hezekiah, Peter* and others whose temptations and falls are recorded for our instruction. Certainly any with a heart for these things will cry, 'How shall I stand, O Lord, if such mighty pillars have been cast to the ground? If such great cedars were blown down, how shall I stand before temptations? Oh, keep me that I do not enter into temptation!' Beholding the footsteps of those who have entered, do you see any that do not have a wound, or at least a blemish?

Paul encourages us on this account to exercise tenderness towards those who have fallen into sin, 'considering ourselves, lest we also are tempted' (*Gal.* 6:1). He does not say 'lest you sin, or fall, or be overtaken with a fault', but, 'lest you are tempted'. As we see the temptation of others, we do not know how soon we too might be tempted, or how we would fare!

Assuredly, he who has seen many stronger men failing, and being cast down in trial, will seek to avoid the battle at all costs. Is it not madness for a man that can barely crawl up and down since he is so weak (which is the case for most of us) if he does not avoid that in which he has seen giants foiled in undertaking it? If you are yet whole and sound, take heed of temptation, lest it happens to you as with Abraham, David, Lot, Peter, Hezekiah, and the Galatians, who fell in time of trial.

The folly of the hearts of men is nowhere shown more openly in the days in which we live than by a cursed boldness and neglect of the warnings of God, and by a lack of consideration of so many that have already fallen into such a sad estate. Yet men run into and put themselves under the power of temptation. They will risk anything, not considering their own weakness, or the concerns of their poor souls. They walk over the dead and slain who have fallen on this path. They see others fall before their eyes, but on they go without regard or trembling! Through this snare hundreds and thousands of professors have fallen within just a few short years.

4. Let us also *consider ourselves* and our great weakness. Let us consider what temptation is, its power, its

effectiveness, and to what it leads. As to ourselves, we are weakness itself. We have no strength or power to withstand. The confidence we have in our own strength adds to our weakness, as it did in Peter. He that boasts he can do anything, can do nothing as he should.

What makes this even worse is that it is a weakness from deception, which is the worst kind of weakness. If a castle is very strong and well fortified, and yet there is a traitor on the inside who is ready to betray it at the first opportunity, that castle is not secure from the enemy. We have traitors in our very heart that are ready to take part and unite against us at every temptation. They will argue for us to give up in the assault; they will even solicit and bribe the temptation to do its work, just as a traitor incites the enemy.

Do not flatter yourself that you can hold out. There are secret lusts that lie dormant, lurking in your hearts, temporarily quiet, waiting for the opportunity of temptation to befall you. They will then rise, argue, cry, disquiet, seduce, with perseverance, until either they are killed or satisfied. He who promises himself that the frame of his heart will be the same under the power of a temptation as it was before is woefully mistaken! 'Am I a dog, that I should do this thing?', says Hazael (2 *Kings* 8:13). Yes, you will be such a dog, if you are ever king of Syria. The temptation of self-interest will break your resolve.

He whose heart currently abhors the thoughts of a particular sin will be powerfully inflamed towards it when he enters into temptation. All contrary reasonings and objections will be overpowered and silenced. He will deride his former fears, cast aside his scruples, and condemn his former convictions. Little did Peter ever think he could so easily deny his Master as soon as he was pressed to admit he knew him. When the hour of temptation came, all resolutions were forgotten and all love to Christ was buried. The present temptation united with Peter's carnal fear and carried all before it.

7

The Folly of Trusting in Our Own Hearts

If we contemplate seeking victory over temptation only in ourselves, what can we expect? All we can look for has to come from our own hearts. What a man's heart is, that the man is. But what is the heart of man worth in a season of temptation?

First, suppose a man is not a believer, but only a professor of the gospel, what can the heart of such a person do? 'The heart of the wicked is little worth' (*Prov.* 10:20). Surely, a heart that is of little benefit for anything will give little help in a time of temptation. A wicked man may be of great use in external things, but if he trusts in his own heart, it is a false hope and will come to nothing. Temptation is heart work, and when temptation comes in like a flood, how can a rotten trifle such as a wicked man's heart stand before it?

Secondly, let us consider the benefit of a heart in any condition. Proverbs 28:26 says, 'He that trusteth in his own heart is a fool.' Trusting in oneself is foolish, no matter the condition of one's heart. This was Peter's error: 'Though all men forsake you, I will not.' This was his folly. Why is trusting in one's heart folly? Because it cannot deliver us! It cannot preserve a man in snares. It will not deliver him in temptation.

The heart of a man will greatly assure him before a temptation comes. 'Am I a dog', said Hazael, 'that I should do this thing?' 'Though all men should deny you', said Peter, 'I will not.' 'Shall I do this evil? It cannot be!' All the arguments that are suitable to strengthen the heart in this matter are mustered up. Do you not think that Peter did this? 'What! Deny my Master, the Son of God, my Redeemer, who loves me? Can such ingratitude, unbelief, rebellion, befall me? I will not do it!'

Shall a man then, rest in his own heart to remain steadfast? Let the wise man answer: 'He that trusts in his own heart is a fool.' 'The heart is deceitful' (*Jer.* 17:9). We would not trust anything in which there is deception and guile, and the heart is just that! It has a thousand shifts and treacheries we must deal with when it enters trial. Every temptation is likely to steal it away (*Hos.* 4:11). A man's heart never fails to deceive him when he places his trust in it.

What are some of the defences the heart seeks to use in the hour of temptation?

1. *Love of honour in the world.* When a man through his former profession and example has accrued a good reputation and esteem in the church, his heart uses this as

a weapon to defend itself in the hour of temptation. 'Shall such a one as I fly? I, who have had such a reputation in the church of God, shall I now lose it by giving way to this lust and temptation? Shall I yield to this or that public evil?' This consideration is used by some people, and they think it will be a shield and buckler against any assaults that may befall them. They will die a thousand times before they will forfeit the reputation they have in the church of God!

But alas! This is just a small thread to bind the giant of temptation. Remember, one third of the angels of heaven fell (*Rev.* 12:4)! Had they not once shone bright in the heavens? Were they not clearly aware of their own honour, height, usefulness, and reputation? But when the dragon came with his temptation, he cast them down! Great temptations will make men who have only this means of defence to lose interest in their honour and reputation, and yield to the temptation after all. Do we not know of instances of men yet living who have ventured to conform to the wicked, and that after they had had a long and useful profession? In a while they find themselves cast down from the reputation they had with the saints. They have hardened themselves against this, and ended in apostasy (*John* 15:6). This weapon did not keep Judas. It did not keep Hymenæus nor Philetus. It did not keep the angels of heaven. It will not keep us either!

2. *Considerations of shame, reproach, loss, and the like.* This also is used as a defence against temptation. Men do

not fear temptation, since they believe that their fear of shame will safeguard and preserve them. They would not for the world bring shame and reproach upon themselves, and so are little concerned about the possibility of failure. The subtle danger in this weapon is that it applies only to *open sins,* sins that the world might take notice of and abhor. It is of no use at all in certain cases of temptation, such as:

i. Where deception and hypocrisy can be used to cover the sin.

ii. In the case of the more publicly acceptable sins of loose and careless living, so typical in our day.

iii. In the case of things not considered sinful by others, though convicting and sinful to the conscience of the one being tempted.

iv. In the case of heart sins.

This weapon has no effect in these cases. Most forms of temptation will offer innumerable ways in which the heart can gain relief while yielding. Besides, experience shows how easily this cord is broken when once the heart begins to be entangled. Every corner of our land is full of examples of this failure.

3. *The resolve not to wound one's conscience.* Men say they do not want to disturb their peace, and bring themselves in danger of hell fire. Surely this, if anything, will preserve them in the hour of temptation! They will not throw away their peace nor endanger their souls by defying God and forfeiting the protecting hand of his

providence. What can be a more effective or prevailing weapon? I confess that this is very important. It should be considered more than it is! Oh, that we might lay more weight upon the preservation of our peace with God than we do! Yet even this consideration is not enough to preserve a person who is off his spiritual guard, and does not follow the other rules I have laid down. Consider three reasons for concern, even with this powerful weapon:

i. The peace of such a person may be a *false peace* or security which is made up of presumption and false hope. This may even be so for a believer. Such was David's peace after his sin, before Nathan came to him. Such was Laodicea's peace, though she was ready to perish, and Sardis's peace, though she was dead! How can a soul have confidence that this weapon will keep him safe when he is not labouring to persevere in Christ's Word and to be watchful in all things? Do you think that the peace that many have today will turn out to be true peace at last? Not at all! These shall go alive down to hell, and death will have dominion over them in the morning! If a man's peace is false, can it help in the battle against sin, when it cannot even preserve itself? It will certainly give way at the first vigorous assault of a temptation in its power. Like a broken reed, it will run into the hand of him who leans upon it.

ii. But suppose the peace concerned is a *true and good peace*. When you trust in this weapon alone, the hour of temptation will present many arguments to overcome its

8

Temptation Darkens the Mind

Consider the power of temptation, both from what has been said already of its effects in the saints of old, and from what the Scriptures teach concerning it.

Temptation will *darken the mind,* so that a man will not be able to make a right judgment of things as he did before he entered into it. As the god of this world blinds the minds of the unbelieving so that they will not see the glory of Christ in the gospel (2 *Cor.* 4:4), and as harlotry, wine, and new wine, take away the heart (*Hos.* 4:11), so it is in the nature of every temptation, more or less, to take away the heart, or to darken the understanding of the person being tempted. It does this in three ways.

1. By *fixing the imagination and thoughts* on the object the temptation tends to, Satan diverts the mind away from those thoughts that would strengthen and help the tempted soul. A man is tempted to believe that he is forsaken of God, that he is an object of his hatred, and that he has no interest in Christ. By this craft of Satan, the mind will be so fixed in the consideration of its present

state, and the distress of it, that the man will not be able to appropriate the considerations that would relieve him against the temptation. In such a case, he walks on in darkness without any light. Temptation so possesses and fills the mind with the considerations of itself that it lacks the clarity of thought it might otherwise have had. The things which previously were so clear to the mind come to lose their force and efficacy, so that when others are speaking to such tempted souls of the things which are for their deliverance and peace, they will not understand, and will scarcely even hear a word spoken to them.

2. Temptation can also darken the mind by *a sad entangling of the affections*. When the affections are engaged, they have a strong influence in blinding the mind and darkening the understanding. If any have not considered this before, you need only open your eyes to what is around you, and you will quickly see it! The engagement of the affections clouds the mind and darkens it. Show me a man engaged in hope, love, and fear in connection with temptation, and I shall quickly show you how he is darkened and blinded. In such a state, a man's understanding will be greatly impaired. Though the judgment will not be utterly changed, it will be darkened and rendered too weak to influence the will and affections. Affections set at liberty by temptation will run on in madness. Previous hatred of sin, fear of the Lord, sense of love, and felt presence of Christ crucified all depart and leave the heart a prey to its enemy!

3. Temptation will give *oil and fuel to our lusts*. It will incite, provoke, disturb, and enrage them beyond measure. Offering a lust or a corruption a suitable object, an advantage, or an occasion, will heighten and exasperate it and, for a time, make it wholly predominate. We see this in the fear of Peter, the pride of Hezekiah, the covetousness of Achan, the uncleanness of David, the worldliness of Demas, and the ambition of Diotrephes.

Temptation will lay the reins on the neck of a lust, and put spurs to its sides, so that it may rush forward like a horse into the battle. A man does not know the pride, fury, or madness of a corruption, until it meets with a suitable temptation. What now will a poor soul do? His mind is darkened, his affections entangled, his lusts inflamed and provoked, and his relief defeated. And where will such a condition end?

9

Public Temptations

It should be remembered that temptations may be public or private. Public temptations are such as that mentioned in Revelation 3:10. It was to come upon the world, 'to try them that dwell upon the earth'. This is a combination of persecution and seduction for the trial of a careless generation of professors.

God uses such a trial to revenge the neglect and contempt shown to the gospel on the one hand, and the treachery of false professors on the other. It will certainly accomplish the purpose he has for it. When a lying spirit offered his services to go forth and seduce Ahab that he might fall, God told him that he would persuade the king, and prevail: 'Go forth, and do so' (*1 Kings* 22:22). This was by divine permission, as to his wickedness, but by a divine commission, as to the punishment intended.

When the Christian world was to be given up to folly and false worship for their neglect of the truth, and their naked, barren, fruitless, Christ-dishonouring profession, it is said of the temptation that was to fall upon them that God would send them 'strong delusion, that they should believe a lie' *(2 Thess.* 2:11). In such a case it comes from God in a judiciary manner. It comes in power, and it shall prevail. If the selfish, spiritually slothful, careless, and worldly frame of spirit, which in these days has infected almost the whole body of professors, is to be tested by such a trial, to kill hypocrites, to wound negligent saints, to break their bones, and make them scandalous so that they may be ashamed, will it not have the power and efficacy to do so? Oh, how has the spirit of error progressed among us! From such come those men who delight not to retain God in their hearts, and so he has 'given them up to a reprobate mind' *(Rom.* 1:28).

It is an amazing thing to see persons of a sober spirit, with great pretensions in the ways of God, overcome, captivated, ensnared, destroyed, by weak means, foolish opinions, and imaginations. It would seem impossible that these could lay hold on a sensible, rational man, much less on professors of the gospel, but these weak things will do this work if the power of God makes them effectual.

At times of a strong public temptation, there are those who have been considered godly whose love begins to wax cold *(Matt.* 24:12), and these then begin to cast cold water on the zeal and love of others, who are little by little infected with this poison. They begin to grow negligent, careless, worldly, and in great spiritual need. They begin to please the flesh. At first the more stable believers blame, judge and perhaps reprove them, but in a short time their love also waxes cold, the original edge of conscience softens, and they too begin to conform and are cast into the same mould: 'A little leaven leavens the whole lump.' Paul repeats this saying (*1 Cor.* 5:6; *Gal.* 5:9). He desired us to be aware of this great danger. It is like an infection spreading to the whole body from the bad example of a few. We know how leaven proceeds to permeate the dough silently and unnoticed. If one little piece of leaven, or one bitter root, may endanger the whole, how much more if there are many roots with much leaven scattered abroad!

Would anyone have thought it possible that so many professors should have fallen into the ways of self, of the flesh, and of the world? Consider the worldly compromises, the neglect of family duties and closet duties, the attitudes of pride, ambition, worldliness, and covetousness that abound. How they have turned away after foolish, vain, ridiculous opinions, deserting the gospel of Christ!

Is it not obvious that this has come to pass? And can we not see how it has happened? A few loose, empty professors, who had never more than a form of godliness, turned away from it, and then began to lead others to comply and seek to please the flesh. Little by little this poison reached even the top boughs and branches of our profession, until almost all flesh has corrupted its way. He that does not go along with this wickedness becomes a target for abuse, and is even in personal danger.

Public temptations are usually accompanied with strong reasons and pleas that are very difficult to resist. This powerful influence leads to an underestimating of the evil to which the temptation leads. The temptation, so strengthened, casts down the people of God from their excellency, shears their locks like Samson's, and makes them like other men.

How full the world is of these specious reasonings and pleadings!

1. There is the plea of *liberty and Christian freedom*. I have seen this perverted into a door to sensuality and apostasy. This begins with light conversation, proceeds to a neglect of the Lord's Day and of public and private duties, and ends in slackness and profaneness.

2. There is the *neglect of public concerns*, under the pretence of leaving them to providence and being content with things as they are. In this way things good in themselves are perverted to wretched fleshly compliances and the ruin of all zeal for God and the interest of Christ and his people in the world.

The result of these things, together with ease and plenty, and the elevation and promotion of those professing godliness to high positions, is that we have not only changed places with the men of the world, but we have also taken in their worldly spirit as well.

We are like a colony planted in a foreign country whose manners degenerate from those of the people from whom they came, and become like those among whom they have settled. How soon they forget the customs, manners, and ways of their own people, and are cast into the mould of those where they were planted!

Are we any different from those who went before us? What did they do that we do not also do? And so it has come to pass that prosperity has slain the foolish, and wounded the wise.

10

Private Temptations

Private temptations have been spoken of already. I will add these two points:

1. Private temptations *unite with particular lusts* to gain entrance into the soul, to provide a foundation for sinful action. John tells us that the things that are in the world are 'the lust of the flesh, the lust of the eyes, and the pride of life' (*1 John* 2:16). He speaks of these things as in the world because the people of the world love them, but it is evident that the real issue is one of the heart. The problem is the heart that loves these things.

In Hebrews 4:2, faith and the promises are said to mix with one another. So also lust and temptation mix together, intertwine, and find mutual encouragement. They grow higher and higher by their mutual strength. By this means temptation gets so deep in the heart that no contrary reasonings can reach it.

You will never conquer the temptation until the lust has been killed. It is like leprosy that has infected a building. The building must be demolished, or the leprosy cannot be cured. It is like gangrene that mixes its poison with a limb. It cannot be removed from the place it infects, but both must be cut off together.

In the case of David's temptation to uncleanness, ten thousand considerations might have been given to break the beginning of that temptation, but it had already united itself with lust, and nothing but the killing of that lust could give him the victory. This deceives many a person. Some have seen a pressing temptation that, having gained some advantage, has become urgent upon them. They have prayed against it, and opposed it with many powerful arguments. Any one of these seems sufficient to conquer and destroy it, or at least to overpower it, so that it should not give any further trouble, but this is not enough. The ground given over is not taken back. The power of it grows upon them more and more.

What is the reason for this? It is that the temptation has incorporated and united itself with the lust, and is safe from all the opposition they use to curb it. If they are to make progress, they must deal with the lust itself. They must address their ambition, pride, worldliness, sensuality, or whatever it might be, that the temptation has united with.

All other ways of dealing with it are like a superficial treatment of gangrene. The whole body might be preserved for a while, though in great torment, but death will come at last. The soul also may torture itself for a season with such a procedure, but it must come to this in the end: the lust must die, or the soul must die!

2. The lust in question, united with the temptation, *seeks to control the whole soul* by one means or another, and so to prevent any opposition. Suppose it is a lust of the mind, such as ambition, pride, and the like. This lust of the mind will also seek the agreement of the affections of the heart, so as to draw the heart away from God. The mind promises the heart that both mind and heart will find much contentment and satisfaction in fulfilling the lust in question.

This lust of the mind will not only disable its own reasonings, but it will draw the whole soul into the same frame by various considerations. It promises all of the soul a share in the spoils. So Judas's money, which he first desired because of his covetousness, was to be shared among all his lusts.

If the temptation is of a more sensual nature, and has taken control of the affections, how strongly the affections will fight against the understanding! They will bribe the mind to acquiesce. What arguments, what hopes, they will suggest to gain the mind's support.

In short, nothing more shows the power of a particular temptation, when it has come to its hour, than the way it will use everything, good, bad, or indifferent, even things seemingly alien to it, to gain its end.

We should always remember Satan's purpose and sin's purpose in temptation: it is the dishonour of God, and the ruin of our souls. Consider the outcome of any former temptations that you have had to grapple with. Have they not defiled your conscience, disquieted your peace, weakened your obedience, and clouded the face of God?

Even though the temptation may not have prevailed as to the outward expression of the sin, have you not been baffled, your soul polluted, and your mind grievously perplexed with it? Indeed, did you ever in your experience come away without sensible loss from any contact with a powerful temptation?

Would you ever be willingly entangled again? If you are at liberty now, take heed: if at all possible, do not go that way again, lest something worse should happen to you.

11

Why Must We Fear Temptation?

We have so far presented many considerations that show the importance of the truth proposed, and how important it is that we take care not to enter into temptation. But there are some objections that may quietly insinuate themselves into the souls of men that might make them negligent and careless in this pursuit, even though it is so important and so necessary a matter for all those who wish to walk with God in peace and faithfulness. We will now consider these objections.

OBJECTION 1. Why should we so fear and labour to avoid temptation when James 1:2 says that we are to count it all joy when we fall into various temptations? If I am to consider it a joy, why should I take great pains to avoid it? To this I answer:

i. This is not a line of reasoning that you could apply in everything. Those familiar with the goodness, wisdom, and love of God in his providence will admit that in whatever state we find ourselves we are to rejoice. In James

1:10, the rich man is encouraged to rejoice when he is brought low, but the same rich man will also seek to use all lawful means so as not to be brought to poverty! In most cases, it would be a sin not to work hard to avoid it. It is our responsibility to do the best we can in the place we occupy. If God alters our condition, we are to rejoice in it. If the temptations here mentioned do indeed befall us, we may have cause to rejoice, but not if we find ourselves there by neglect of duty!

ii. The word temptation can be used in two ways. It can be used *passively* and merely regarding circumstances, and thus it is a trial, a testing; or, *actively*, as an enticement to sin. The words in James 1:2 refer to temptation in the first sense only, that of various trials, the testing of faith, and the patience this produces. The same is true of verse 12, which speaks of perseverance under trial, and receiving the crown of life which the Lord has promised to those who love him.

But in the second sense James says: 'Let no man say when he is tempted, I am tempted of God: for God cannot be tempted with evil, neither tempteth he any man. But every man is tempted, when he is drawn away of his own lust, and enticed' (*James* 1:13–14).

So then, though it is a blessed thing when we endure afflictions which God sends upon us for the testing of our faith, we are nevertheless to use all care and diligence that our lusts do not take occasion from or advantage of any temptation to sin which may be presented. This is the sense of the second passage.

OBJECTION 2. But was not our Saviour Christ himself tempted, and is it evil to be brought into the same state and condition as he was? Indeed, it is not only said that he was tempted, but that it was advantageous to us that our high priest should so suffer: 'For in that he himself hath suffered being tempted, he is able to succour them that are tempted' (*Heb.* 2:18). Also, in Luke 22:28, Christ's makes it the foundation of a great promise to his disciples that they stayed with him in his trials. To this I answer:

It is true that our Saviour was tempted, but his temptations are considered part of the *evils* that befell him in the days of his flesh. They were things that came on him through the malice of the world and of the prince of the world. He did not wilfully cast himself into temptation. That would have been to tempt God (*Matt.* 4:7). Our condition is such that, even with the greatest diligence and watchfulness, we surely shall still be tempted, even as Christ was. Even so, it is our duty to do our utmost to avoid falling into temptation.

The reason is this: Christ had only the *suffering* part of temptation when he entered into it. We also have the *sinning* part of it. When the prince of this world came to Christ, he had no claim on him; but when he comes to us, he has a claim on us. In one way, we are like Christ, in that we also experience trials and disturbances, and are instructed to rejoice in them. In another way, we are unlike him, in that we are defiled and entangled by temptation, and should by all means seek to avoid it. We never have the same victory as Christ. Who of us has ever 'entered into temptation' and not been defiled?

OBJECTION 3. What is the point of this great effort and care? Is it not written that God is faithful, and will not allow us to be tempted above what we can bear, but will with the temptation also make a way to escape (*1 Cor.* 10:13)? And does not the Lord know how to rescue the godly from temptations (*2 Pet.* 2:9)? Why then must we be so careful that we do not enter into temptation?'

I answer:

I much question what assistance someone will have from God in temptation if he willingly enters into it just because he supposes God has promised to deliver him out of it. The Lord knows that, even when we have done our utmost to avoid them, we shall still enter into various temptations through the craft of Satan, the trickery and malice of the world, and the deceitfulness of sin. In his love, care, tenderness, and faithfulness, he has provided the sufficiency of his grace for us that these shall not utterly prevail to make an everlasting separation between him and our souls. But I still have three things to say concerning this objection.

i. He who wilfully or negligently enters into temptation has no reason in the world to promise himself any assistance from God, or any deliverance from the temptation into which he has entered. The promise is made to those who meet temptation in their way, and not to those who go out of their way to meet with it. Therefore, the devil (as is often observed) when he tempted our Saviour, even by quoting Scripture (*Matt.* 4:6), left out part of the the text, 'in all thy ways' (*Psa.* 91:11). The promise of deliverance is to those who are 'in their ways'. A principal feature of these ways is to beware of temptation!

ii. Even though there is the sufficiency of grace provided for all the elect, so that they will never utterly fall from God in any of their temptations, to think of the dishonour to God, the scandal to the gospel, and the woeful darkness and disturbance they will bring upon their own souls, is enough to make any gracious heart to tremble, even though they do not perish. Those who are not influenced by these considerations, but only by the fear of hell, in my estimation have more reason to fear it than perhaps they are aware of.

iii. To approach temptation on the basis that you believe God will protect you is the same as continuing in sin that grace might abound (*Rom.* 6:1–2). This thought the apostle rejects with the greatest detestation.

Is it not madness for a man to willingly allow the ship he is sailing in to split itself on a rock, to the irrecoverable loss of his merchandise, just because he supposes he shall, in his own person, safely reach the shore on a plank?

Is it any less madness for a man to hazard the shipwreck of all his comfort, peace, joy, the glory of God, and the honour of the gospel he is entrusted with, merely on the supposition that his soul shall yet escape?

12

Knowing Our Danger

Three particular cases arise from a general consideration of these things. The first is, How may someone know that he has entered into temptation?

1. *When a man is drawn into any sin*, he may be sure that he has entered into temptation. All sin is the result of temptation (*James* 1:14). Sin is a fruit that comes only from that root. Even though a man is suddenly or violently surprised by any sin, yet it sprang from some temptation or other. Paul says that if a man is surprised, or overtaken with a fault, we should restore such a one, but watch ourselves, lest we also are tempted (*Gal.* 6:1). Therefore, when a man is surprised and taken unawares, as it were, temptation was the cause of it.

Some do not take notice of this, to their great disadvantage. When they are overtaken with a sin, they set themselves to repent of that sin, but they do not consider the temptation that was the cause of it. They should set themselves against this as well, and take care that they do not enter into it any more. Otherwise they are quickly entangled by it again, even though they have the greatest possible hatred of the sin. He who seeks to get the victory over any sin must also consider his temptation to it, and strike at that root. Without deliverance from this, he will not be healed.

This is a folly that traps many who have lively sense of sin. They are sensible of their *sins*, but not of their *temptations*. They are displeased with the bitter fruit, but cherish the poisonous root. Hence, in the midst of their humiliation for sin, they will continue in the ways, the society, and the pursuit of the ends that have provided the occasion for their sin.

2. *Some temptations are of such violence as to leave us in no doubt what we have to wrestle with.* They rise to such a height, press so heavily on the soul, so torture and disturb it, that their nature is clear. When a fever rages, a man knows he is sick. The lusts of men, as James tells us, entice or draw them to sin, and this can happen without peculiar instigation, in a quiet, even, and sedate manner. But if the temptation grows more violent, if it hurries the soul up and down, giving it no rest, we may know for certain that temptation is assisting and strengthening the lust.

Just as an empty vessel in a stream that flows to the sea will infallibly be carried there, according to the course and speed of the stream, so men's lusts will infallibly (if not mortified in the death of Christ) carry them into eternal ruin. Often this happens without much noise, according to the course of the stream of their corruptions. But let the wind of strong temptations fall on them and they are hurried into innumerable scandalous sins, broken by the waves, and swallowed up in eternity.

In the same way Hezekiah had the root of pride in him always, yet it did not make him run up and down to show his treasure and riches until he fell into temptation through the ambassadors of the king of Babylon. David was able to avoid numbering the people until Satan stood up and provoked him and solicited him to do it. Judas was covetous from the beginning, but he did not contrive to satisfy his covetousness by selling his Master until the devil entered into him, and he entered into temptation. The same thing might be said of Abraham, Jonah, Peter, and the rest. When any lust or corruption violently disturbs the soul, you may know that your lust is being strengthened by some outward temptation, and that you must take heed to it more than ordinarily.

3. Lesser degrees of temptation may also be detected. For instance, *when the heart begins secretly to enjoy the matter of the temptation*, and is willing to feed and to increase it in any way it can without outright sin, the soul is entering into temptation

Thus a man may begin to have a reputation for piety, wisdom, learning, or the like, and to be much spoken of in that regard. If his heart is tickled to hear of it, and his pride and ambition are affected by it, and he now, with all his strength, seeks to increase these things so that he may shine among men, he has entered into temptation. If he continues to follow this path, he will quickly become a slave of lust.

So it was with Jehu. He saw that his reputation for zeal began to grow, and his honour on account of it. Then Jonadab came along, a good and holy man. 'Now', thought Jehu, 'I have an opportunity to grow in honour for my zeal.' So he called Jonadab to him, and went to work in earnest. The things he did were good in themselves, but he had entered into temptation because he served his lust in all that he did.

So it is with many scholars. They come to be esteemed and favoured for their learning. This then takes hold of the pride and ambition of their hearts. They determine to set themselves to study with all diligence day and night; a good thing in itself, but they do it to satisfy the thoughts and words of men in which they delight. In all they do, they are making provision for the flesh to fulfil its lusts.

It is true God will often bring light out of this darkness, and turn things to a better outcome. When a man has studied for years with the wrong motive, rising early and going to bed late, to satisfy his lusts, God may come in with his grace, and turn the soul back to himself. God then robs those Egyptian lusts, which had been devoted to idols, and consecrates them for use in his tabernacle!

Men may also become entangled like this in even better occupations, some in the profession of piety, others in their labour in the ministry, etc. A man's profession can also become a snare, such as his reputation and honour for disciplined labour. In our day of party spirit, some who have become honourable in their labours for their party will secretly glory in it and become entangled. They will press into it with more than ordinary diligence and activity to elevate their honour even more. They need rather to lie in the dust with a sense of their own vileness. This temptation is so appealing that often it does not even need food to feed its lust. He who is entangled with it might avoid the means and ways of honour and reputation, whispering in his heart that such avoidance will achieve honour in itself.

The same may be true even in the preaching of the gospel and the work of the ministry. Many things in the ministry might yield esteem: ability, plainness, faithfulness, success; and all may become fuel for temptations. If such a one, because he enjoys the praise which is feeding his lust, seeks to increase it, either by things good in themselves, or at least not downright sinful, he has entered into temptation.

4. *Whenever a man's state or condition in life, or any other circumstance, gives opportunity for his lust to be stirred up and provoked*, let that man know, even though he does not yet see it, that he has certainly entered into temptation.

To enter into temptation, as we have seen, is not merely to be tempted, but to be under the strong power of temptation and to be entangled with it. It is almost impossible for a man to have opportunities and occasions presented to him which are well suited to his lust and corruption and not to be entangled. When the ambassadors came from the king of Babylon, Hezekiah's pride cast him into temptation. When Hazael became king of Syria, his cruelty and ambition made him rage savagely against Israel. When the priests came with their thirty pieces of silver, the covetousness of Judas sprang instantly to work to sell his Master.

Many illustrations even in our present day could be given. Some men think that they can play on the hole of the asp and not be stung, touch pitch and not become dirty, take fire in their clothes and not be burnt, but they are greatly mistaken. If your business, course of life, social position, or anything else, is cast upon you in such a way as to suit your lust or corruption, know that you have entered into temptation. How you will fare in such a case, only God knows.

Take the example of a man that has any seeds of filthiness in his heart engaged in the course of his life in society which is light, vain or foolish: even if he takes little notice of it, or none at all, he has undoubtedly entered into temptation.

So it is also with ambition in high places, passion in a multitude of perplexing affairs, polluted corrupt delights in vain company, or the perusal of idle books or treatises of vanity and folly. Fire and combustible material may more easily be placed together without affecting each other than particular lusts and suitable objects or occasions for their exercise.

5. When a man, contrary to his former frame of mind, *becomes weak, negligent or formal in his duties,* when he can omit duties or content himself with a careless, lifeless performance of them, without delight, joy, or satisfaction to his soul; let him know that, though he may not be acquainted with the particular cause of his failure, for one reason or another he has entered into temptation. In time, the source will become evident, to his trouble and peril.

How many have we seen in our day who, from a warm profession, have fallen to be negligent, careless, indifferent in praying, reading, hearing, and the like! Give me an instance of one who has emerged without being wounded in the process, and I dare say you may find a hundred who have been asleep on the top of a mast. They have been captivated in some vile temptation or other, and it has brought forth bitter fruit in their lives and ways.

A few who have returned from their folly complain, 'Oh! I neglected private prayer; I did not meditate on the Word, nor attend to hearing it, but rather I despised these things; and yet I said I was rich and lacked nothing. Little did I consider that this unclean lust was ripening in my heart; and that this atheism, and these abominations were alive and multiplying there!'

This is a certain rule: If a man's heart grows cold, negligent, or formal in his duties and in the worship of God, either as to the matter or the manner of them, and this is different from his former manner, then one temptation or other has laid hold upon him. The world, pride, uncleanness, self-seeking, malice, envy, or one thing or another has possessed his spirit; grey hairs are here and there upon him, though he does not perceive it.

This is to be observed in the manner of his duties as well as in the matter. Men may, for many devious reasons, especially for the satisfaction of their consciences, keep up and maintain the duties of religion, as to the substance and matter of them, when they have no heart for them, or no life in them. They lack spiritual life in their performances, and are therefore 'dead' (*Rev.* 3:1).

As it is in the sickness of the body, if a man finds his spirit faint, his heart oppressed, or his head heavy, the whole person is affected, and even if he does not have a temperature, yet he will cry, 'I fear I am getting a fever, I am so out of order and unwell.' A man may do so also in the sickness of the soul. If he finds his pulse is not beating properly and evenly towards his duties of worship and communion with God, if his spirit is low, and his heart fainting, let him conclude that, though his lust does not yet burn or rage within him, he has entered into temptation.

It is high time for him to consider the particular cause of his disease. If his head is heavy and sleepy in the things of grace, if his heart is cold in duties, evil lies at the door. If such a soul escapes a great temptation to sin, yet he shall not escape a great testing through the Lord leaving him. In the Song of Solomon 5:2, the spouse cries, 'I sleep', and says that she has put off her coat and cannot put it on; she has an unwilling disposition, as to her duties and her communion with Christ. What happens next? In verse 6, her Beloved has withdrawn himself. Christ has gone; and though she seeks him she cannot find him!

There is such a close agreement between the new nature that is wrought and created in believers and the duties of the worship of God that they will not be parted or hindered unless by the interference of some disturbing disease. The new creature feeds upon these spiritual duties and is strengthened and increased by them. He finds sweetness in them and meets with his God and Father in them. He so delights in them and desires to engage in them that the only thing that will keep him from them is if he is made sick by some temptation. This attitude of spiritual thirst is expressed in Psalm 119 throughout. The soul will not be cast out of this frame of mind unless it is oppressed and disordered by one secret temptation or another.

There are also many other evidences of entering into temptation which the soul may discover if it searches into them, but I mention these to remove the false security to which we are so prone.

13

Means of Preservation

The second particular enquiry arising from our consideration of temptation is, What are the best means to preserve us from entering into temptation? We have already seen the instructions given by our Saviour in Matthew 26:41. He sums up everything in these two words, 'WATCH and PRAY.' I shall seek to show what is wrapped up in these words.

1. These words imply *a clear, abiding awareness of the great evil of entering into temptation.*

The reason a man watches and prays against something is because he considers it evil and by all means to be avoided. This brings us to the *first direction*, namely, *Always bear in mind the great danger of entering into temptation.* It is sad to think that most do not consider this important. They are content to avoid the actual outbreak of sin. All sorts of men venture all the time on any temptation in the world. Thus young men will go into any company or society. At first they are delighted with evil company, and before long they are delighted with the evil itself. How vain are all warnings to them to beware of such persons who themselves live in sinful excess and delight in the corruption of others. They are destroyers of souls! At first young men join in their company while abhorring the thought of practising their lewdness; but where does it lead? Except for one here or there whom God snatches with a mighty hand from the jaws of destruction, most are lost. After a while, they fall in love with the evil which at first they abhorred. This open door to the ruin of souls is very evident. Sad experience also makes it clear that it is almost impossible to make many poor creatures fear the temptation, though they profess to fear and hate sin.

How many professing believers have I known that plead for their *liberty,* as they call it! They proceed to hear any opinion from any person; they seek to try all things, whether they come to them in the ways of God or not. They run to hear every teacher of false and abominable opinions, and every seducer, though condemned by the saints in general.

Yes, they are free to hear them, though they claim to hate their views. But what is the outcome? I have hardly known any who have come away without a serious wound. The faith of most is overthrown. Let no man then pretend to fear sin that does not fear temptation also! These two are too closely united to be separated. Satan has put them together, so that it is very hard for any man to separate them. He does not truly hate the fruit who delights in the root.

When men see that certain ways, types of company, courses of action, studies, and aims, will entangle them, make them cold and careless, quench their zeal, indispose them to consistent and universal obedience, and yet still go on with them, sin lies at the door. Only a tender frame of spirit, aware of its own weakness and corruption, the craft of Satan, the evil of sin, and the power of temptation, can enable someone to do his duty. And until we bring ourselves to this frame of mind we shall never free ourselves from sinful entanglements. Boldness to venture into temptation for various specious reasons has ruined countless professing Christians in these days. It continues to cast many down from their excellency. Nor have I any hope for a more fruitful profession among us until I see more fear of temptation. Sin will not long seem great or weighty to any who consider temptation a light or small thing.

The first thing wrapped up in this general direction, then, is to exercise our thoughts daily with the great danger of entering into temptation. Grieving the Spirit of God, disturbing the peace of our own souls, losing our peace, and risking our eternal welfare, are at stake. If anyone is not convinced of the importance of observing this direction, all that follows will be of no value. If temptation is not feared, it will conquer. But if the heart is made tender and watchful in this, half the battle of living a consistent Christian life is won. Anyone who does not resolve to put this direction into practice daily and conscientiously need read no further.

2. The second thing wrapped up in the general direction is that *keeping ourselves from entering into temptation is not a thing in our own power.* We are to pray that we might be preserved from it because we cannot keep ourselves.

This is a further means of preservation. Just as we have no strength to resist a temptation when it comes, without a supply of sufficient grace from God, so to realize that we do not have the power or wisdom to keep ourselves from entering into temptation is a preserving principle. We are in all things kept by the power of God (*1 Pet.* 1:5)! Our Saviour shows us this, not only by instructing us to pray for deliverance from entering into temptation, but by his own intercession for us to be kept from it (*John* 17:15).

He prayed that we might be spared from that which is in the world, the temptations in the world, all the evil in the world, and the evil one himself, who uses the things of the world in his temptations. Christ prays to his Father to keep us, and instructs us also to pray that we might not enter into temptation. It is therefore not something we can do in our own power.

The ways of our entering into temptation are many, various, and imperceptible, the means are very powerful, and its entrance is deceitful, subtle, imperceptibly gradual, and plausible! Our own weakness and our lack of watchfulness are so great that we cannot in the least degree keep or preserve ourselves from it. We lack both wisdom and power for this work.

Let the heart, then, commune with itself and say, '*I am poor and weak*; *Satan* is subtle, cunning, powerful, watching constantly for advantages against my soul; the *world* is earnest, pressing, and full of persuasive pleas with innumerable false and deceitful claims; my own corruptions are violent, disturbing, enticing, entangling – conceiving sin, and warring in me and against me! Moreover, there are countless occasions and opportunities for temptation in everything I do or suffer. The beginnings of temptation are almost imperceptible and so agreeable to me that, if I were left to myself, I would not even know that I was trapped until my bonds were made strong and sin had gained ground in my heart. Therefore I will rely on God alone for my preservation, and continually look up to him for it.'

This will make the soul commit itself always to the care of God, resting on him, and undertaking nothing without asking his counsel.

Observing this direction results in a double advantage to the soul in its preservation from the evil feared:

i. *It engages the grace and compassion of God*, who calls the fatherless and helpless to rest on him; for the soul who, in a sense of need, rolls itself on him, on the basis of his gracious invitation, never fails to receive fresh supplies.

ii. *Keeping the soul in this frame of spirit greatly tends to its preservation*, for he who looks to God for help in this way is both aware of his danger and careful to use means for his preservation.

3. This also is wrapped up in the general direction, that we should *exercise faith in the promise of God for our preservation*. To believe that God will preserve us is a means of preservation, for this he certainly will do, or else he will make a way for us to escape out of temptation if we fall into it with such a believing heart. We are to pray for what God has promised. Our requests are to be regulated by his promises and commands, which are both of the same extent. Faith takes God's promise to itself and so finds relief. James instructs us concerning believing prayer. What we lack we must ask of God, but we must 'ask in faith', for otherwise we must not suppose that we will receive anything from the Lord (*James* 1:5–7).

This, then, is also contained in the direction of our Saviour to watch and pray, lest we enter into temptation: that we should exercise faith in the promises of God to preserve us from temptation. He has promised to keep us in all our ways, that we shall be directed in a way in which, though we are fools, we shall not go astray (*Isa.* 35:8), that he will lead us, guide us, and deliver us from the evil one. If we set faith to work on these promises of God, we may expect a good and comfortable outcome. We can hardly conceive what a train of graces attends faith when it goes forth to meet Christ in the promises, and what a power for the preservation of the soul lies in this very thing. But I have spoken of this elsewhere.[1]

---

[1] See *The Mortification of Sin* (Edinburgh: Banner of Truth, 2004; ISBN 0 85151 867 2, 144 pp., pbk.), especially Chapter 14.

14

Praying for Protection

We will consider the two parts of our Saviour's instruction separately, and first *his instruction to pray*.

To pray that we should not enter into temptation is a means to preserve us from it. All men that know anything of prayer speak glorious things of this duty, yet the truth is that not one half of its excellency, power, and effectiveness is known.

It is not my business here to treat prayer in general, but I must say this in regard to my present purpose, *Let him who would spend little time in temptation spend much in prayer*. Hebrews 4:16 teaches us what suitable help and mercy are laid up for us in Christ, to be obtained through prayer. Prayer puts our souls into a posture of opposition to every temptation. In Paul's instruction to put on the whole armour of God, so as to resist and stand firm in the time of temptation, he adds this at the end, 'Praying always with all prayer and supplication in the Spirit . . . with all perseverance and supplication' (*Eph.* 6:18).

Without prayer the rest of the armour will be of no value; therefore consider what weight he lays on it. We are to pray at all times and seasons, always ready and prepared for the discharge of that duty (*Luke* 18:1).

Paul adds, 'with all prayer and supplication in the Spirit': uttering all kinds of desires that are suited to our condition before God, according to his will, and assisted in this by the Spirit. And we are to be alert and watchful in this, so as not to be diverted by anything whatsoever, and persevere in it to the very end. In this way we shall stand firm. The soul thus engaged is in a healthy posture.

Without prayer, this important work will not be accomplished. If we do not continue in prayer, we shall continue in cursed temptations. Let this, then, be a further direction: *Abide in prayer, with the express purpose of not entering into temptation.*

Let this be part of our daily wrestling with God, that he would preserve our souls, and keep our hearts and our ways, so that we should not be entangled; that his good and wise providence would so order our ways and our affairs that no pressing temptation should befall us; and that he would give us diligence, care, and watchfulness over our own ways. In this way we shall be delivered when others are held fast with the cords of their own folly.

15

Watching in Seasons of Special Danger

The other part of our Saviour's instruction, *to watch*, is more general. I shall consider some things contained in it; and first, *the seasons in which men more usually enter into temptation.*

There are many times in which the hour of temptation is particularly near, and in which it will certainly seize the soul, unless we are delivered by God's mercy, as a result of watchfulness. At such a time we must be particularly on our guard to avoid the power of temptation. Consider several dangerous seasons:

1. *A season of unusual outward prosperity* is usually accompanied with an hour of temptation. Prosperity and temptation go together; indeed, prosperity *is* a temptation, or many temptations in one, and without particular supplies of grace it is apt to lay the soul open to any assault and provide fuel and food for all. It provides both for lust and for the darts of Satan.

Solomon tells us that 'the prosperity of fools shall destroy them' (*Prov.* 1:32). It hardens them in their way, makes them despise instruction, and ignore the coming of the evil day that should influence them to amendment. Without special assistance, even believers find prosperity to carry an inconceivably malignant influence upon them. Agur prays against riches, because of the temptation that accompanies them; 'Lest', he said, 'I be full and deny thee, and say, Who is the LORD?' (*Prov.* 30:8–9), forgetting the Lord, as God complains that his people did (*Hos.* 13:6). David was mistaken in this way also. 'In my prosperity I said, I shall never be moved' (*Psa.* 30:6). All was well, but what lay just ahead, David had not considered: 'Thou didst hide thy face, and I was troubled.' God was ready to hide his face, and David was about to enter into a temptation of desertion, though he did not know it.

As to a prosperous condition, I shall not contradict Solomon's counsel to be joyful in the day of prosperity (*Eccles.* 7:14). We should rejoice in the God of our mercies, who is so good to us in his patience and forbearance, notwithstanding all our unworthiness. Yet we need to add another word, from the same fountain of wisdom: 'Consider' also, lest evil is near. A man in such a state is in the midst of snares. Satan has many advantages against him, and is forging darts out of all his enjoyments. If he does not watch, he will be entangled before he is aware.

If you lack that which provides poise and ballast to your heart, formality in religion will be likely to creep upon you, and lay open your soul to all temptations in their full power and strength. Satisfaction and delight in creature comforts can poison the soul, and are apt to grow upon you. We must be vigilant and circumspect, or we will be taken by surprise. Job says that in his affliction God made his heart soft (*Job* 23:16). There is a hardness, an imperceptible lack of spiritual understanding, received in prosperity. If it is not watched against, it will expose the heart to the deceits of sin and the baits of Satan. 'Watch and pray' in this season. It has cost many men dear to neglect this. Their sorrowful experiences cry out to us to take heed. Blessed is he that fears temptation always, but especially in a time of prosperity.

2. Another dangerous season is *a time when grace sleeps*, when communion with God is neglected, or when duty is only formal. Then one must watch, for certainly some other temptation will accompany it.

Let a soul in such a state wake up and look around him. His enemy is near, and he is ready to fall into such a condition as may cost him very dear all the days of his life. His present state is bad enough in itself; but it is also a serious indication that something worse is lying at the door. The disciples that were with Christ in the garden had not only a physical drowsiness but also a spiritual drowsiness upon them. What does our Saviour say to them? 'Arise; watch and pray, that you enter not into temptation.' We know how near one of them was to his bitter hour of temptation and, since he was not watching, as he should, he immediately entered into it.

I already mentioned the spouse in the Song of Solomon 5:2–8. She slept, was drowsy, and was unwilling to gird herself up to a vigorous performance of duties, in the way of quick, active communion with Christ. Before she was aware, she had lost her Beloved. Then she moaned, questioned, cried, and endured pain and reproaches, before she obtained him again. Consider then, poor soul, your state and condition! Does your light burn dim? Or if it gives others just as great a blaze as it did formerly, you may not see the face of God in Christ as clearly as you did before (2 *Cor.* 4:6). Is your zeal cold? Even though you are doing the same works as formerly, and proceeding in the same course, is your heart as warmed with the love of God as it has been formerly? Do you neglect praying or hearing? Are you observing them with the life and vigour that you formerly did? Are you flagging in your profession? If you do keep it up, are your wheels oiled by some ulterior motives from within or without? Does your delight in the people of God grow faint and cold? Or is your love for them changing from that which is purely spiritual into that which is very carnal and in accord with the principles of the natural man, if not something worse?

If you are in such a drowsy condition, take heed; you are falling into some sorrowful temptation that will break all your bones, and give you wounds that will remain with you all the days of your life. Yes, when you awake you will find that it has laid hold of you already, and you did not know. It has smitten and wounded you, and you did not complain or seek relief and healing.

This was the state of the church of Sardis. The things that remained were about to die (*Rev.* 3:2). 'Wake up,' says our Saviour, 'and strengthen them.' See also John 5:14: 'Sin no more, lest a worse come unto thee.' If any reading this finds himself in this condition, and if he has any regard for his poor soul, let him now awake, before he is entangled beyond recovery. Take this warning from God, and do not despise it.

3. *A season of great spiritual enjoyments* may, by the malice of Satan and the weakness of our hearts, be turned into a season of danger with respect to temptation.

We know how it was with the apostle Paul (2 *Cor.* 12:7). He had glorious spiritual revelations of God and Jesus Christ. Instantly Satan fell upon him, a messenger from him buffeted him. Paul pleaded for its departure, but he was left to struggle with it. God is pleased sometimes to give us special discoveries of himself and his love and to fill our hearts with his kindness. Christ takes us into the banqueting-house and gives our hearts their fill of his love. By a special work of his Spirit he overpowers us with a sense of his love in the unspeakable privilege of our adoption, and so fills our souls with joy unspeakable and full of glory.

A man would think that this was the securest condition in the world. In such a moment, what man does not cry out with Peter on the mountain, 'It is good for me to be here; to abide here for ever'? But very frequently some bitter temptation is now at hand. Satan sees that since we are possessed by such a joy, we quickly neglect many ways of access to our souls. Satan seeks to find and take advantage of these against us. When God at any time gives us to drink of the rivers of pleasure that are at his right hand, and satisfies our souls with his kindness as with marrow and fatness, let us not say, 'We shall never be moved.' We do not know how soon God may hide his face, or a messenger from Satan may buffet us.

Besides, there is often a greater and worse deception in this business. Men cheat their souls with their own fancies instead of a true sense of God's love by the Holy Spirit. They feel safe and secure in God's love, but in reality are lifted up with their own imaginations. They then find relief against what their consciences are telling them in the foolish imagining and self-deception with which they entertain themselves. How fearfully they are exposed to all manner of temptation! Do we not see this every day: persons walking in the vanities and ways of this world, yet boasting of their sense of the love of God? Shall we believe them? If so, we must disbelieve truth itself! How sorrowful, then, must their condition be.

4. A fourth season is *a season of self-confidence*. In such a time temptation is usually at hand.

The case of Peter illustrates this: 'I will not deny you; though all men should deny you, I will not; though I were to die for it, I would not do it.' Peter said this at the very time when he stood on the brink of the temptation that would cost him bitter tears. This taught him to know himself all his days, and gave him such an understanding of the state of all believers that when he later received more of the Spirit and of power, yet he had less confidence in himself, and so persuaded all men to 'pass the time of their sojourning here in fear' (*1 Pet.* 1:17). He did not wish them to be confident and proud as he had been, lest they fall as he fell. Peter had put himself above all the others: 'Though all men should forsake you, yet I will not.' He suspects every man's loyalty more than his own. But when, after the resurrection, our Saviour puts a direct comparison to him: 'Simon, son of Jonas, lovest thou me more than these?' (*John* 21:15), Peter has had enough of comparing himself with others and only cries, 'Lord, you know that I love you.' He will not lift himself up above others any more.

Seasons of self-confidence often beset us. Though temptations are everywhere, with false doctrines and innumerable other allurements and provocations all around, we are very confident that we shall not be taken in by them. Though all men should fall into these follies, yet we will not. We will never depart from our walking with God. It is impossible that our hearts should be so foolish. But the apostle says, 'Let him that thinketh he standeth take heed lest he fall' (*1 Cor.* 10:12).

Who would think that Peter, who walked on the sea as Christ did, confessed him to be the Son of God, and was with him on the Mount of Transfiguration when he heard the voice from the excellent glory, would immediately fall into cursing and swearing that he did not know him, at the word of a servant girl? There was no legal inquisition after him, no judicial process going on. Let all who are at all inclined to watch against sin beware of self-confidence!

This is the first important part of watching: consider the seasons in which temptation usually makes its approach to the soul, and arm yourself against them.

16

Watching Our Hearts

We have considered watchfulness with respect to the outward means, occasions, and advantages that temptation uses. We now proceed to consider the heart itself. Watching or *keeping the heart* is one of our greatest obligations. To perform this rightly, consider the following directions:

DIRECTION 1. *If you would avoid entering into temptation, labour to know your own heart*. Become acquainted with your own spirit, natural temperament, lusts and corruptions, and natural, sinful, or spiritual weaknesses. By finding where your weakness lies, you may be better able to keep at a distance from all occasions of sin.

Our Saviour told the disciples that they did not know what manner of spirit they were of when they, under a pretence of zeal, displayed ambition and vengefulness (*Luke* 9:54–55). If they had been aware of it, they would have watched over themselves. David tells us that he considered his ways and kept himself from the iniquity to which he was particularly prone (*Psa.* 18:23).

Temptation often takes an advantage from a man's natural temper and constitution. Some are naturally gentle, cooperative, easily entreated, pliable. Though this is the noblest natural temperament, and the best and choicest ground, when well prepared and watered, for grace to grow in, yet if not watched over, it will be a means of countless unforeseen entanglements in temptation. Others are gruff, hard to please, gloomy, so that envy, malice, selfishness, resentment, hard thoughts of others, and complaining are at the very threshold of their natures. These can scarcely step out but they are in the snare of one or other of these. Others are very passionate, and so on. We need to be aware of our own natural tempers, so as to watch out for the treachery that lies in them.

You may have a Jehu in you that will make you drive furiously; or a Jonah, that will make you ready to complain; or a David, that will make you hasty in your decisions. He who does not watch these things carefully will always be entangled in one temptation or another.

And just as men have different natural temperaments which, as they are watched and managed, can provide either fuel to sin or an occasion for the exercise of grace, so they may also have particular lusts or corruptions which, through their natural constitution, education, or other factors, become strongly rooted in them. These also need to be understood. Unless we know and are alert to these, they will continually entangle and ensnare us.

Labour, then, to know yourself, what manner of spirit you are of, what agents Satan has in your heart, where corruption is strong, where grace is weak, what strongholds lust has in your natural constitution, and so on.

How many have had all their comforts blasted and their peace disturbed by their natural passion and fretfulness! How many have been rendered useless in the world by their unreasonableness and discontent! How many are snared even by their own gentleness and easy-going attitude! Be acquainted, then, with your own heart. Though it is deep, search it out. Though it is dark, enquire into it. Though it gives other names to all its faults than those they deserve, do not believe it!

Because men are utter strangers to themselves and put flattering labels on their natural faults, because they seek to justify, extenuate, or excuse the evils of their own hearts that suit their natural tempers and constitutions, instead of seeking to destroy them, and so prevent themselves from having a clear and distinct view of them: for these reasons they hang all their days in the same briers and make no attempt to get free. Uselessness and scandal in professors are the result of this lack of acquaintance with their own frame and temper. How few there are who will either diligently study themselves, or else bear with those who seek to make them better acquainted with themselves!

DIRECTION 2. When you know the tendencies of your heart in the respects mentioned, *watch against every kind of occasion, opportunity, activity, society, solitude, or business that tends to entangle your natural temperament, or that provokes your corruption.*

It may be that there are some situations, some kinds of society or business, in which you have never in your life been able to escape the temptation that arises, because it is so suitable to ensnare or provoke your particular corruption. It may be that you are in a state and condition of life that wearies you every day on account of your ambition, passion, discontent, or the like. If you have any love for your soul, it is time for you to awake and deliver yourself, as a bird from an evil snare. Peter would not be in a hurry to come again to the high priest's house, nor would David again walk on the top of his house when he should have been out on the battlefield. It would be impossible to enumerate all the specific instances in which this could apply, since they are so various, as the natures of different persons vary. Whatever it is, we should avoid it, not pass by it, turn away from it and pass on (*Prov.* 4:14–15).

Awareness of these dangerous occasions is a significant part of the wisdom needed to order our behaviour rightly. Since we have so little power over our hearts when they meet a suitable provocation, we are to keep heart and provocation apart, as a man would keep fire away from the combustible parts of his house.

DIRECTION 3. *Be sure to lay up provisions in store against the approach of any temptation.* This is a part of our watchfulness over our hearts. You may ask, 'What provision do you mean, and where is it to be laid up?' Our heart is our treasury, as our Saviour calls it (*Matt.* 12:35). There we lay up whatever we have, good or bad;

and from there we can draw it out for our use. The heart is where provision is to be laid up against temptation. When an enemy approaches a fort or castle to besiege and take it, often, if he finds it well-manned, furnished with provisions for a siege, and well able to hold out, he withdraws and does not assault it. If Satan, the prince of this world, comes and finds our hearts fortified against his weapons, with ample provisions to hold out, he not only departs, but as James says, he flees: 'He will flee from you' (*James* 4:7).

As for the provision to be laid up, it is what is provided for us in the gospel. Gospel provisions will do this work: that is, they will keep the heart full of a sense of the love of God in Christ. This is the greatest preservative in the world against the power of temptation.

Joseph was prepared in this way, so that, on the first appearance of temptation, he cried out, 'How can I do this great wickedness, and sin against God?' (*Gen.* 39:9). That was the end of the temptation. It was not able to lay hold of him, but departed. He was furnished with such a ready sense of the love of God that the temptation could not stand before it. The love of Christ controls us, says the apostle, so that we should live for him (2 *Cor.* 5:14–15) and so withstand temptation.

A man ought also to lay in store the provisions of the law: fear of death, hell, punishment, and the terror of the Lord in them. But these are far more easily conquered than the gospel provisions, and they will never be able to stand alone against a vigorous assault. Law provisions are overcome every day. Hearts trusting in them alone will struggle for a while, but quickly give up.

Store up in your hearts a sense of the love of God in Christ, the eternal purpose of his grace, the savour of the blood of Christ, and his love in the shedding of it; get a taste for the privileges we have through this: our adoption, justification, acceptance with God; fill your hearts with thoughts of the beauty of holiness, as the effect Christ intended in dying for us; and you will, in the ordinary course of walking with God, have great peace and security from the disturbance caused by temptations.

When men can live and plod on in their profession, and not be able to say when they last experienced any living sense of the love of God or of the privileges they have in the blood of Christ, I do not know how they can keep themselves from being ensnared.

The apostle tells us that the peace of God will keep our hearts (*Phil.* 4:7). The word *keep* is a military word and means to *garrison*. A garrison has two features: it is exposed to the assaults of its enemies; but there is safety in it from these attempts. It is so with our souls. They are exposed to temptations and assaulted continually. If they are surrounded by a garrison, temptation shall not enter, and consequently we shall not enter into temptation. Now, how is this to be done? The peace of God shall do it. What is this peace of God? It is a sense of his love and favour in Jesus Christ. Let this abide in you, and it shall garrison you against all assaults whatever. Besides, there is in this sense of love and favour that which is in direct opposition to all the ways and means that temptation uses to approach our souls. Striving to obtain and keep a sense of the love of God in Christ, by its very nature, undermines all the workings and insinuations of temptation. Therefore, lay up a store of gospel provisions which will make the soul a place of defence against all the assaults of temptation.

17

Watching for the Approach
of Temptation

A further aspect of watching relates to *being aware of the first approach of temptation.* The following directions are intended to help in this:

DIRECTION 1. *Always be alert, so that you may discover your temptations early and recognize them for what they are.* Most men do not perceive their enemy until they have already been wounded. Others looking on may see that they are in the thick of battle, but they themselves are oblivious! They are like men asleep, with no sense of danger, until others come to tell them their house is on fire.

Temptations approaching through something neutral, which may or may not be used in this way, are particularly hard to discern. Few take notice of it until it is too late. Then they find themselves entangled, if not wounded. Watch, then, so as to understand the snares that are laid for you early, and to see the advantages your enemies have against you before they gather strength and power, before the temptation becomes united with your lusts and infuses poison into your soul.

DIRECTION 2. *Consider the aim and tendency of the temptation, whatever it is, and the objectives of all concerned in it.* The two active agents in your temptation are Satan and your own lusts. I have shown elsewhere that what your lust always aims at is the very worst of evils. It never acts but out of a settled enmity against God. Therefore look on it from the very start as your mortal enemy, whatever its pleas to the contrary. 'I hate it', says the apostle (*Rom.* 7:15); that is, the working of lust in me. 'I hate it; it is the greatest enemy I have. Oh, that it were killed and destroyed! Oh, that I were delivered from its power!' Since it is your sworn enemy that is approaching you, it would be the height of madness to throw yourself into his arms to be destroyed. But I have spoken more of this in my work on Mortification.[1]

And does Satan have any more friendly an aim and intention towards you? Is he not a participant in every one of your temptations? His kind of friendship is to beguile you as a serpent, and devour you as a lion. I shall only add that when he tempts you to do something which is against the law, that is not his real aim. What he is really attacking is your interest in the gospel. He is only using sin as a bridge to get over to a better ground to assault you. He may say today, 'You may venture on sin,

[1] See footnote on p. 66.

because you have an interest in Christ', but tomorrow he will be telling you in no uncertain terms that you have no interest in Christ because of what you have done.

DIRECTION 3. *Meet your temptation at the outset with thoughts of faith concerning Christ on the cross;* this will make temptation sink before you. Have no negotiations, no arguments with it, if you would escape it. Say, 'It is Christ that died', that died for sins such as these. This is called taking up the shield of faith, to quench the fiery darts of Satan (*Eph.* 6:16). Faith is able to do this by laying hold on Christ crucified, his love in dying, and his suffering on the cross for sin. Whatever your temptation is, whether to sin, or to fear or doubting on account of sin, or about your state and condition, it cannot stand before faith lifting up the standard of the cross. We know how the Papists, who have lost the power of faith, keep up the form, and cross themselves or make the sign of the cross in the air, thus thinking to scare away the devil. But to exercise faith in Christ crucified is truly to sign ourselves with the sign of the cross, and by this means we shall overcome that wicked one (*1 Pet.* 5:9).

18

When Surprised by Temptation

But suppose the soul has been surprised by temptation, and entangled unawares, so that it is now too late to resist its first approaches? What should such a soul do to avoid being plunged deeper and carried away by its power?

1. *Do as Paul did, plead with God again and again that it may depart from you* (2 Cor. 12:8). If you continue in this, you will certainly either be speedily delivered out of the temptation, or else receive sufficient grace not to be completely foiled by it. But do not even think about the things you are tempted to. This often leads to further entanglements. Set yourself against the temptation itself. Pray against it, that it may depart. And when the temptation is taken away, you may more calmly consider the things themselves.

2. *Flee to Christ in a particular way, since he was also tempted, and beg of him to give you help in this time of trouble and need.* The apostle tells us that, having been tempted himself, he is able to help those who are being

tempted (*Heb.* 2:18). The meaning is this: When you are tempted and ready to faint, when you need help—you must have it or you will die—place your faith particularly on Christ as he was tempted. That is, consider that he was tempted himself, that he suffered as a result of it, that he conquered all temptations, and that he did so, not merely on his own account, but (since it was for our sakes he submitted to be tempted) for us. He conquered in and by himself, but it was for us. Expect help from him (*Heb.* 4:15–16). Lie down at his feet, and make your complaint known to him. Beg his assistance, and it will not be in vain.

3. *Look to him who has promised deliverance.* Consider that he is faithful, and will not suffer you to be tempted above what you are able to bear. Consider that he has promised a happy outcome to all these trials and temptations. Call to your mind all the promises of assistance and deliverance that he has made. Ponder them in your heart. And rest upon this, that God has countless ways that you know nothing of to bring about your deliverance. Consider, for example, that:

i. He can *send an affliction* that will mortify your heart with respect to the matter you are tempted about, whatever it is, so that what was before a sweet morsel under your tongue will have neither taste nor relish to you. Your desire for it will have been killed, as was the case with David.

ii. He can by some providence *alter the whole state of affairs from which a temptation arises,* so that, the fuel being taken away, the fire will go out by itself. This also happened to David in the day of battle.

iii. He can *tread down Satan under your feet*, in such a way that he will not dare to suggest any thing more to your disadvantage. The God of peace will do this, so that you shall hear nothing more from Satan.

iv. He can *give you such a supply of grace that you may be freed*, although not from the temptation itself, yet *from the tendency and danger of it*, as was the case with Paul.

v. He can *give you such a comfortable persuasion of good success in the eventual outcome of your trials* that you will have refreshment in them and be kept from the trouble of the temptation, as was the case also with Paul.

vi. He can *utterly remove the temptation, and make you a complete conqueror.* And he has innumerable other ways of keeping you from entering into temptation and protecting you from being foiled by it.

4. *Consider how the temptation which surprised you made its entrance.* Search this out and with all speed repair the breach. Stop up the channel by which the waters were able to enter. Deal with your soul like a wise physician. Enquire when, how, and by what means you fell into this disease. And if you find that negligence, carelessness, or lack of keeping watch over yourself was the root of it, concentrate on that. Mourn over it before the Lord, repair that breach, and then proceed to the work that lies before you.

19

Keeping the Word of Christ's Patience

All the directions considered so far are partly given in various places in the Scripture and partly arise from the nature of temptation itself. But there is one general direction which is comprehensive of all that has gone before, while also adding to what we have already considered. It contains an approved antidote against the poison of temptation and is a remedy that Christ himself has marked out with a guarantee of efficacy and success. It is given us in the promise of our Saviour himself to the church of Philadelphia:

Because they have kept the word of his patience, says he, he also will keep them 'from the hour of temptation, which shall come upon all the world, to try them that dwell upon the earth' (*Rev.* 3:10).

Since Christ is the same yesterday, today, and forever, as he dealt with the church of Philadelphia, so he will deal with us. If we keep the word of his patience, he will keep us from the hour of temptation.

This, then, is a way of rolling the whole care of this weighty affair on the One who is able to bear it, and so it requires our particular consideration.

I will, therefore, show, 1. *What keeping the word of Christ's patience is,* so that we may understand our duty, and 2. *How this will be a means of our preservation,* so that we may be established in faith in Christ's promise.

1. What is keeping the word of Christ's patience?

i. *What is the word of Christ?* The word of Christ is the word of the gospel, the word revealed by him from the bosom of the Father. It is the word of the Word, the word spoken in time by the eternal Word. It is therefore called 'The word of Christ' (*Col.* 3:16), or 'the gospel of Christ' (*Rom.* 1:16; *1 Cor.* 9:12), and 'the doctrine of Christ' (*Heb.* 6:1). 'Of Christ', that is, as its Author (*Heb.* 1:1–2), and of him as the chief Subject of it (*2 Cor.* 1:20).

ii. *Why is this called 'the word of Christ's patience'?* It is called the word of Christ's patience, or tolerance and forbearance, because of the patience and long-suffering which he exercises towards the whole world, and all persons in it, in the dispensation of the gospel. For he is patient:

a. *Towards his saints.* He bears with them and suffers from them. He is 'patient toward us' (*2 Pet.* 3:9), that is, those who believe. The gospel is the word of Christ's patience even to believers. Anyone acquainted with the gospel knows that there is no attribute of Christ rendered more glorious than that of his patience. That he bears with so much unkindness, so many unnecessary breaches, so much neglect of his love, so many affronts to his grace, and so many violations of our promises shows that the gospel is not only the word of his grace, but also the word of his patience. Christ also suffers *through* his people in the reproaches they bring on his name and ways, and he suffers *in* them, for 'in all their afflictions he was afflicted'.

b. *Towards his elect not yet effectually called.* In Revelation 3:20, he stands waiting at the door of their hearts and knocks for an entrance. He deals with them by all means, and yet stands and waits until his 'head is filled with dew, and his locks with the drops of the night' (*Song of Sol.* 5:2), as if enduring the cold and inconveniences of the night so that when the morning is come he may have entrance. Often for a long time they scorn him in his own person, persecute his saints and his ways, and revile his word, while all the while he stands at the door in the word of his patience, his heart full of love towards their poor rebellious souls.

c. *Towards the perishing world.* For this reason the time of Christ's kingdom in this world is called the time of his 'patience' (*Rev.* 1:9). He endures the vessels of wrath with much long-suffering (*Rom* 9:22). While the gospel is administered in the world he is patient towards the men of the world, until the saints in heaven and earth are astonished and cry out, 'How long?' (*Psa.* 13:1-2; *Rev.* 6:10). He is patient while men mock him as if he were an idol (*2 Pet.* 3:4). He endures bitter things from them, with respect to his name, ways, worship, saints, promises, threats, all his interest of honour and love, and still is forbearing with them, lets them alone, and does them good. Nor will he cut this way of proceeding short until the gospel is no longer preached. Patience must accompany the gospel.

iii. *What is implied in keeping the word of Christ's patience?* Three things are implied: *knowledge, valuation,* and *obedience.*

a. *Knowledge.* He who will keep this word must know it in four respects: as a word of *grace* and *mercy,* to save him; as a word of *holiness* and *purity,* to sanctify him; as a word of *liberty* and *power,* to enable him and set him free; as a word of *consolation,* to support him in every condition.

1. *As a word of grace and mercy, able to save.* It is 'the power of God unto salvation' (*Rom.* 1:16). 'The grace of God . . . bringeth salvation' (*Titus* 2:11). The word of grace that is 'able to build us up, and to give us an inheritance among all them that are sanctified' (*Acts* 20:32). 'The word . . . is able to save our souls' (*James* 1:21). When someone knows the word of the gospel as a word of mercy, grace, and pardon, as the sole evidence for life, and as the conveyance of an eternal inheritance, he will strive to keep it.

2. *As a word of holiness and purity, able to sanctify.* 'Ye are clean through the word which I have spoken unto

you', said our Saviour (*John* 15:3). This is why he prayed as he did in John 17:17. He who does not know the word of Christ's patience as a sanctifying and cleansing word, in its power on his own soul, neither knows nor keeps it. Those with an empty profession in our day do not know the first step toward this duty. That is why most are overcome by the power of temptations. And yet men full of self, of the world, of anger, ambition, and almost all unclean lusts, still speak of keeping the word of Christ (see *1 Pet.* 1:2; *2 Tim.* 2:19)!

3. *As a word of liberty and power, to ennoble him and set him free,* not only from the guilt of sin and from wrath, for it does that as a word of grace and mercy; and not just from the power of sin, for it does that as a word of holiness; but it delivers him from all outward servility to men or the world that might entangle him or enslave him. It declares us to be Christ's freemen, not in bondage to any (*John* 8:32; *1 Cor.* 7:23).

We are not freed by it from due subjection to superiors, nor from our duty, nor are we free to sin (*1 Pet.* 2:16). But in two respects it is a word of freedom, liberty, largeness of mind, power, and deliverance from bondage: in respect of conscience, as to the worship of God (*Gal.* 5:1), and in respect of ignoble slavery to men and things in the world, in the course of our pilgrimage. The gospel gives a free, large, and noble spirit, subject to God, but to nothing else! It gives a spirit 'not of fear, but of power, and of love, and of a sound mind' (*2 Tim.* 1:7); a mind 'in nothing terrified' (*Phil.* 1:28), not swayed by others for any reason.

There is nothing more unworthy of the gospel than a mind in bondage to persons or things, prostituting itself to the lusts of men or the fear the world inspires. The one who knows the word of Christ's patience in reality and power is freed by it from countless temptations, impossible to describe.

4. *As a word of consolation, to support him in every condition,* and to be a full portion, whatever else is lacking. It is a word attended with 'joy unspeakable and full of glory'. It gives support, relief, refreshment, satisfaction, peace, consolation, joy, boasting, and glory in every possible situation.

Thus to *know* the word of Christ's patience, the gospel, is the first part, and a great part, of fulfilling this condition of being kept from the hour of temptation.

b. *Valuation.* Keeping this word also involves valuing it. It is to be kept as a treasure. It is that excellent deposit that is to be kept by the Spirit who dwells in us (2 *Tim.* 1:14). The apostle also says, 'Hold fast the faithful word' (*Titus* 1:9). It is a good treasure and a faithful word: hold it fast! It is a word that holds within it the whole interest of Christ in the world. To value it as our greatest treasure is to keep the word of Christ's patience. Those who want Christ to look on them in the time of temptation must look to what concerns him now!

c. *Obedience.* Personal obedience, in keeping all the commands of Christ, is the keeping of his word (*John*

14:15). Adhering closely to him in holiness and universal obedience, in those times when the opposition the gospel of Christ meets with in the world makes it distinctly the word of his patience, is the very life and soul of the duty we are speaking of.

Now, when all these are carried out with determination of mind and spirit, care of heart, and diligence of the whole person, we are keeping the word of his patience indeed.

The sum, then, of this duty, which is the condition of freedom from the power of temptation, is to have a due acquaintance with the gospel as a word of mercy, holiness, liberty and consolation, to value it and everything that relates to it as one's choice and only treasure, and to make it the business of one's life to pursue universal obedience to Christ, especially when opposition and apostasy stretch the patience of Christ to the utmost. Wherever we fall short of this, there temptation is sure to enter.

20

A Sure Preservative

I come now to show, in the second place, the connection between our keeping the word of Christ's patience and our preservation in the day of temptation.

2. *That keeping the word of Christ's patience is a sure means of our preservation appears in these points:*

i. *This text alone gives us the promise of preservation.* It was given as a solemn promise in this regard to the church of Philadelphia. A great trial and temptation was to come on the world at the opening of the seventh seal (*Rev.* 7:3), but judgment could not proceed till the servants of God were sealed in their foreheads. These are those who keep the word of Christ, for the promise is that it should be so.

Now, in every promise there are three things to consider: the *faithfulness* of the Father, who gives the promise; the *grace* of the Son, which is the content of the promise; and the *power and efficacy* of the Holy Spirit, who puts the promise into effect.

a. *The faithfulness of God* accompanies the promise. Our deliverance is based on this (*1 Cor.* 10:13). Though we are tempted, yet we shall be kept from the hour of temptation. It shall not grow too strong for us. That which comes upon us we shall be able to bear, and that which would be too hard for us, we shall escape. What security do we have for this? The faithfulness of God: 'God is faithful, who will not suffer you . . .' And where is God's faithfulness seen and exercised? 'He is faithful that promised ' (*Heb.* 10:23). His faithfulness consists in the discharge of his promises. He remains faithful; he cannot deny himself (*2 Tim.* 2:13). In being under a promise, we have the faithfulness of God engaged for our preservation.

b. In every promise of the covenant there is *the grace of the Son.* He is the subject-matter of all promises! He promises, 'I will keep you.' How? 'By my grace with you.' So that whatever assistance the grace of Christ can give a soul that has a right to this promise, in the hour of temptation that soul shall have it. Paul's temptation grew very great, and would probably have prevailed, but he besought the Lord, that is the Lord Jesus Christ, for help (*2 Cor.* 12:8). The answer he received was, 'My grace is sufficient for thee' (verse 9). We know that it was the Lord Jesus Christ and his grace that Paul had to do with for at the close of that verse he said; 'I will glory in my infirmities, that the power of Christ may rest upon me', that is, that the efficacy of the grace of Christ in his preservation should be made evident. See also Hebrews 2:18.

c. *The efficacy of the Spirit* also accompanies the promises. He is called 'the Holy Spirit of promise', not only because he was promised by Christ, but also because he effectually makes good the promises of God, and accomplishes them in our souls. The Spirit also, then, is engaged to preserve the soul walking according to the rule that has been laid down. See Isaiah 59:21.

Thus, wherever the promise is, there is all this assistance: the faithfulness of the Father, the grace of the Son, and the power of the Spirit. All three are engaged in our preservation!

ii. *The constant, universal keeping of the word of Christ's patience keeps the heart and soul in such a state that no temptation, no matter how great an advantage it may have, will be able to prevail.* So David prays: 'Let integrity and uprightness preserve me' (*Psa.* 25:21). Integrity and uprightness are the Old Testament counterpart of keeping the word of Christ and walking closely with God. But how can they preserve a man? Why, by keeping his heart in such a frame that, defended on every side, no evil can approach or take hold of him. If a man fails in his integrity, he opens the door for temptation to enter.

To keep the word of Christ is to do it universally, as we have seen. This exercises grace in all the faculties of the soul, and surrounds it with the whole armour of God. The understanding is full of light, and the affections full of love and holiness. Whatever direction the wind blows from, the soul is defended and fortified. Whenever and by whatever means the enemy assaults, everything in the soul of such a one is on guard. The defence is ready, 'How can I do this thing, and sin against God?'

There are two particular reasons why deliverance and safety arise from this keeping of the word of Christ's patience:

a. *It mortifies the heart to the matter of temptation.* A temptation is able to prevail in the heart because the heart is ready to fall in with the temptation. There are lusts in our hearts that are well suited to the proposals of the world and Satan. James therefore reduces all temptations to our own lusts (*James* 1:14), since they either proceed from them or are made effectual by them. Why do danger or threats turn us aside from the faithful performance of our duty? Is it not because of unmortified carnal fear in us that rises up at such a season? Why do the allurements of the world and compromises with worldly men entangle us? Is it not because our affections are already entangled with the things and considerations proposed to us?

Now, keeping the word of Christ's patience, in the manner we have described, keeps the heart dead to these things, and so it is not easily entangled by them. 'I am crucified with Christ', says Paul (*Gal.* 2:20). He that keeps close to Christ is crucified with him, and is dead to all the desires of the flesh and the world, as appears more fully in Galatians 6:14. Here is where the match is broken off, and all entangling love dissolved. The heart is crucified to the world and everything in it. The matter of almost all temptations is taken from the world, the men of it, and the things in it. But as for these things, says the apostle, 'I am crucified to them', and so is everyone who keeps the word of Christ; as if to say, 'My heart is mortified to them. I have no desire nor affection for them, no delight in them, and they are crucified unto me. The crowns, glories, thrones, pleasures, profits of the world, I see nothing desirable in them. The lusts, sensual pleasures, love, respects, honours of men, name and reputation among them, they are all as nothing to me. I do not value them, nor estimate them highly.' Such a soul is safe from the assaults of manifold temptations. When Achan saw the beautiful Babylonish garment, the two hundred shekels of silver, and the wedge of gold, first he coveted them, then he took them (*Josh.* 7:21). So temptation subtly spreads the Babylonish garment of favour, praise, and peace, the silver of pleasure or profit, and the golden contentments of the flesh before the eyes of men. If there is a corresponding lust alive in the heart, still unmortified, it will break out in covetousness. Whatever fear of punishment there may be, the heart or the hand will still be put forth to iniquity.

Herein lies the safety of the frame of spirit described. It is always accompanied by a mortified heart, crucified to the things that form the subject-matter of our temptations. Without this it is utterly impossible that we should be preserved for one moment when any temptation falls upon us. If fondness and love for the things that are proposed, insinuated, or commended by the temptation are still living and active in us, we shall not be able to resist or stand!

b. *In this frame, the heart is filled with better things.* A sense of their excellency fortifies us against the entrance of any temptation. See what resolution this gives rise to in Paul: everything is loss and refuse to him (*Phil.* 3:8). Who would go out of his way to have his arms filled with loss and refuse? And how does Paul come to have such an estimation of the most desirable things in the world? It is because of the very high estimation he had of the excellency of Christ. As we see in verse 10, when the soul is engaged in communion with Christ, and walking with him, he drinks new wine, and cannot desire the old things of the world, for he says, 'The new is better!' He tastes every day how gracious the Lord is, and so does not pine for the sweetness of forbidden things, which really have none. He who makes it his business to eat daily of the tree of life will have no appetite for other fruit, even if the tree that bears them seems to stand in the midst of paradise.

The spouse in the Song of Solomon made this the means of her preservation, that is, she set the excellency which she found in Christ and his graces in daily communion above all other desirable things. Let a soul, then, exercise itself to a communion with Christ in the good things of the gospel, the pardon of sin, the fruits of holiness, the hope of glory, peace with God, joy in the Holy Spirit, dominion over sin, and it shall have a powerful protection against all temptations. Just as the full soul loathes the honeycomb (*Prov.* 27:7), and a soul filled with carnal, earthly, sensual contentments will find no relish or savour in the sweetest spiritual things, so he that is satisfied with the kindness of God, as with marrow and fatness, who is every day entertained at the banquet of wine upon the lees, well refined (*Isa.* 25:6), has a holy contempt of the enticements and allurements that lie in prevailing temptations, and so is safe!

21

Considerations That Keep Us Safe

A third way in which keeping the word of Christ's patience is a sure means of preservation is that *he who does so is always furnished with considerations and principles that tend to his preservation,* with moral and real advantages to that end.

i. *Preserving considerations.* These powerfully influence his soul in his walking diligently with Christ, in addition to his sense of duty, which he always has. He considers:

a. *The concern that Christ, whom he loves, has about him and the careful way he is seeking to walk.* He remembers that the presence of Christ is with him, and his eye upon him; that he ponders his heart and ways, as one greatly concerned with how he will act in a time of trial (see Revelation 2:19–23). He takes everything into consideration, what is acceptable and what is to be rejected. The soul knows that Christ is concerned for his honour, lest his name should be evil spoken of on his account; and that he has a loving concern for him, having the firm intention of presenting him holy, blameless and beyond reproach in his presence (*Col.* 1:22). The Spirit too, he knows, is grieved when Christ is interrupted in this work. The soul knows that Christ is concerned for his gospel, its progress, and its reception in the world. Its beauty would be slighted, its good things reviled, and its progress hindered if temptations prevailed. Others too might be grievously scandalized, and perhaps even ruined, if those professing the gospel were overpowered by temptation. When Hymenæus and Philetus fell they overthrew the faith of some.

Because of this, when intricate, confusing, entangling, temptations arise, whether public, private, or personal, the soul that seeks to keep the word of Christ's patience will say, 'Shall I now be careless? Shall I be negligent? Shall I comply with the world and its ways? Oh, what thoughts concerning me has the One whose eye is upon me! Shall I slight his honour, despise his love, trample his gospel in the mire under the feet of men, turn aside others from his ways? Shall such a man as I fly, and give up fighting? It cannot be!' He who keeps the word of Christ's patience is full of such soul-pressing considerations. They dwell in his heart and spirit, and the love of Christ constrains him to keep his heart and his ways (2 *Cor.* 5:14).

b. *The temptations of Christ on his behalf, and his victory over all assaults for his sake and God's.* The prince of this world came upon him and everything in earth and hell that had any allurement or terror in it was proposed to him to divert him from the work of mediation which he had undertaken on our behalf. He called his whole life the time of his 'temptations' (*Luke* 22:28), but he resisted all, conquered all, and became the Captain of salvation to all who obey him. The tempted soul therefore says, 'Shall this temptation, these arguments, this plausible pretence, this sloth, this self-love, this sensuality, this bait of the world, prevail over me to desert him who went before me in the way of every temptation that his holy nature could be subject to, for my good?'

c. *Sorrowful thoughts of what it would be like to lose the love of Christ and the smiles of his countenance* also exercise such a soul. He knows what it is to enjoy the favour of Christ, to have a sense of his love, to be accepted in coming to him, and talking with him. Perhaps he has sometimes lost this, and knows what it is to be in the dark and at a distance from him. In the Song of Solomon, when the spouse has found her Beloved again, she holds him; she will not let him go; she is determined never to lose him (*Song of Solomon* 3:4).

ii. *Preserving principles:* He who keeps the word of Christ's patience is moved by preserving principles.

a. He lives by *faith* in all things and is governed by it in all his ways (*Gal.* 2:20). Now faith, put into practice, has the power to preserve from temptation, first because it empties the soul of its own wisdom, understanding, and sufficiency, so that it may act in the wisdom and sufficiency of Christ. In trials and temptations, Solomon advises us to trust in the Lord with all our hearts and not to lean to our own understanding (*Prov.* 3:5). This is the *work* of faith; it *is* faith; it is to *live* by faith. The great cause of men falling into trials is their leaning to, or leaning upon, their own understanding and counsel. What is the outcome of this? 'The steps of his strength shall be straitened, and his own counsel shall cast him down' (*Job* 18:7). First he shall be entangled, and then cast down, and all by his own counsel, until he becomes ashamed of it, as was Ephraim (*Hos.* 10:6).

If we consult our own understanding in our trials, and listen to our own reasonings, though they seem to be good and to tend to our preservation, yet the principle of living by faith is stifled, and the outcome will be to be cast down by our own counsel. Nothing can empty the heart of this self-sufficiency but faith: living by faith, not living to ourselves, but having Christ live in us by our living by faith on him.

By making the soul poor, empty, helpless, and destitute in itself, faith engages the heart, will, and power of Jesus Christ for assistance.

b. The second preserving principle is *love to the saints.* A concern that the saints should not suffer because of us greatly tends to preserve us in times of temptation and trial. We see how powerful this motive was in David in his earnest prayer, 'Let not them that wait on thee, O

Lord GOD of hosts, be ashamed for my sake: let not those that seek thee be confounded for my sake, O God of Israel' (*Psa.* 69:6), as if to say, 'O let me not so go wrong that those for whom I am willing to lay down my life should be put to shame, be evil spoken of, dishonoured, reviled, scorned on my account, for my failings!' A selfish soul whose love is turned wholly inward will never be able to abide in a time of trial.

Will it not now be easy to see why it is that so many, in our days, are overcome in the time of trial; why the hour of temptation brings them down before it? Is it not that so few among the great multitude of professors keep the word of Christ's patience? If we wilfully neglect or cast away our interest in this promise of preservation, is it any wonder that we are not protected?

An hour of temptation has come upon the world, to try those who dwell there. It exerts its power and efficacy in various ways. There is nothing in which it may not be seen acting and exerting itself: in worldliness, sensuality, loose conversation, neglect of spiritual duties, both private and public, in foolish, loose diabolical opinions, in pride and ambition, envy and wrath, strife and debate, revenge, selfishness, atheism and contempt of God. These are all branches from the same root, bitter streams from the same fountain, favoured by peace, prosperity, security, and apostasies of professing Christians. And, alas! How many daily fall under the power of this temptation! How few are like pilgrims, with garments undefiled! And if any particularly pressing temptation comes, how few escape! May we not describe our condition as the apostle does that of the Corinthians, 'Some are sick, and some are weak, and many sleep?' Some are wounded, some defiled, and many utterly lost. What is the spring and fountain of this sad state of things? Is it not as we have said: We do not keep the word of Christ's patience in a consistent, careful walk with him, and so we lose the benefit of the promise attached to this course of action?

If I should try to summarize the ways in which professors come short of keeping the word of Christ, it would be a lengthy task, but four categories would contain most of them:

1. *Conformity to the world* from which Christ has redeemed us. In almost everything they rejoice and delight to conform to the men of the world.

2. *Neglect of duties* which Christ has instructed us in, from meditation in secret to public worship.

3. *Strife, disagreements, and debates among ourselves*, with wretched judging and despising of one another over things that are nothing to do with the bond of communion that should be among the saints.

4. *Self-sufficiency* as to principles, and *selfishness* as to ends.

Now, where these things prevail, are men not carnal? Is the word of Christ's patience working powerfully in them? Will they be preserved? They will not.

22

Help in Watching
against Temptation

If you seek to be preserved and kept from the hour of temptation, consider the following cautions and applications which can be deduced from what has already been said.

1. *Beware of relying on your own counsel, understanding, and reason.* Though they seem very plausible in your defence, they will leave you and betray you. When the temptation comes to any height, they will turn on you and take the side of your enemy. They will plead as much in support of the temptation, whatever it is, as they did against it before.

2. *Beware of relying even on your most strenuous efforts in such methods as prayer and fasting against a particular lust or temptation.* These will not help you if, in the meantime, you are negligent in other areas. A man may wrestle, cry, and struggle over a particular temptation, and then immediately give way to worldly ways,

worldly conformity, looseness and neglect in other things. It would be only right if the Lord Jesus Christ were to leave such a person in the hour of temptation.

3. *Beware of using the truths of the perseverance of the saints and preservation from total apostasy to fight particular temptations.* Every kind of security that God gives us is good in its own way, and for the purpose for which it is given. When it is given for one purpose, it should not be used for another. To make use of the general assurance of preservation from total apostasy to support the spirit in respect of a particular temptation will not in the end be advantageous to you. You may be protected from apostasy, but this or that temptation may still prevail. Many have tried this approach, only to find themselves in deep perplexity.

As well as taking heed to these cautions, make use of the great provision of protection that lies in keeping the word of Christ's patience in the midst of all trials and temptations. In particular:

1. *Give careful consideration to the ways in which the word of Christ's patience is most likely to suffer in the days in which we live,* and set yourself vigorously to keep his word in that particular respect. You will say, 'How shall we know in what respects the word of Christ's patience is likely to suffer at any particular time?' I answer, Consider what works Christ seems particularly to be engaged in at a given time, and the neglect of his word

with respect to these will show in what ways his word is likely to suffer. The works in which Christ seems to have been particularly engaged in our day are these:

i. *Pouring contempt on the great men and the great things of the world, and all its enjoyments.* He has brought to light the barrenness of all earthly things in overturning, overturning, overturning both men and things, to make way for the things that cannot be shaken (see *Ezek.* 21:26–27).

ii. *Distinguishing between his own people and the world,* claiming them as his own inheritance, putting a difference between the precious and the vile, and causing his people to dwell apart and not be reckoned among the nations (see *Num.* 23:9).

iii. *Drawing near to faith and prayer,* and honouring them above all the strength and counsels of the sons of men (see *James* 4:8).

iv. *Recovering his ordinances and institutions from the carnal administrations that they were in bondage under* through the lusts of men, bringing them forth in the beauty and power of the Spirit (see *Heb.* 9:10, *1 Pet.* 4:2).

In what ways, then, does the neglect of the word of Christ's patience show itself at such times? Is it not in:

i. *Overvaluing the world and the things of it,* which Christ has stained and trampled under foot?

ii. *Slighting God's people;* treating them as if they were just the same as the men of the world?

iii. *Relying on our own counsels and understanding,* instead of faith and prayer?

iv. *Defiling his ordinances;* giving the outer court of the temple to be trodden upon by unsanctified persons (see *Rev.* 11:12)?

Let us then be watchful, and in these things keep the word of Christ's patience, if we value our own preservation.

2. *In this frame of spirit urge upon the Lord Jesus Christ his own blessed promises,* with all the considerations that may be apt to hold the King in his galleries (see *Song of Sol.* 7:5), and may work on the heart of our blessed and merciful High Priest to give suitable help in our time of need.

23

General Exhortations

Having considered the duty of watching that we enter not into temptation, I suppose I hardly need to add motives for the observance of it. Those who are not moved by their own sad experiences, nor by the importance of the duty itself, as laid down at the beginning of this discourse, I must leave to the further patience of God. I shall only conclude the matter with a general exhortation to those who are in any measure prepared for it by the considerations that we have advanced.

If you went into a hospital and saw many persons lying sick and weak, sore and wounded, with many foul diseases, and asked them how they fell into this condition, and they all agreed that such and such a thing was the occasion of it: 'By that I got my wound', says one; 'And my disease', says another; would it not make you somewhat careful how or what you had to do with that thing or place? Surely it would!

Or if you went into a dungeon and saw many miserable creatures bound in chains for an approaching day of execution, and asked them how they were brought into that condition, and they should all fix on one and the same thing, would you not take care to avoid it? The case is so with entering into temptation. Ah! How many poor, miserable, spiritually wounded souls, have we everywhere! One wounded by one sin, another by another; one falling into filthiness of the flesh, another of the spirit. Ask them how they came into this estate and condition. They must all answer, 'Alas! We entered into temptation, we fell into cursed snares and entanglements; and that has brought us into the sad condition you see!'

And if a man could look into the dungeons of hell and see the poor damned souls that lie bound in chains of darkness, and hear their cries, what would he learn there? What do they say? Are they not cursing their tempters and the temptations that they entered into? And shall we be negligent in this thing?

Solomon tells us that the simple one that follows the strange woman knows not that the dead are there, that her house leads to death, and that her paths lead to the dead (which he repeats three times); and that is the reason why the simple venture into her snares. If you knew what has been done by entering into temptation, you would be more watchful and careful. Men may think that they will fare well enough without this concern; but, 'Can a man take fire in his bosom, and his clothes not be burnt? Can one go upon hot coals, and his feet not be burnt?' (*Prov. 6:27–28*). It is not possible! Men will not come out of their temptation without wounds, burns, and scars.

I do not know any place in the world where there is more need of pressing this exhortation than this place.[1] Go to our various colleges, enquire for such and such a young man. What is the answer concerning many? 'Ah, he was very hopeful for a season; but he fell into ill company, and he is quite lost. Another started off well in religion, we expected great things from him, but he has fallen into temptation.' And so in other places: 'He was useful and humble, and adorned the gospel; but now he is so sadly entangled with the world that he is living for self, and has no life and savour. Such and such a person was humble and zealous; but he has advanced, and has lost his first love and ways.' Oh! How full is the world, how full is this place, of such mournful examples, to say nothing of those innumerable poor creatures who have fallen into temptation by religious delusions. Is it not time for us to awake before it is too late, to watch against the first rising of sin, the first attempts of Satan, and all the ways in which he has made his approaches to us, even if they are never so harmless in themselves?

Do we not have our own experiences of weakness, folly, and the invincible power of temptation when once it has got within us? Finally, as for this duty of watching that I have insisted on, consider:

1. *If you neglect the only means prescribed by our Saviour, you will certainly enter into temptation, and just as certainly fall into sin.* Do not flatter yourselves. Some

---

[1] The discourses were originally delivered in Oxford.

of you are 'old disciples', you have a great hatred of sin, you think it is impossible that you should ever be seduced in such and such a way, but, 'Let him [whoever he is] that thinks that he stands, take heed lest he fall.' No grace you have received, no experience you have had, no resolution you have formed will preserve you from any evil; you must stand upon your guard: 'What I say to you', says Christ, 'I say to all, Watch!' Perhaps you may have had a good measure of success for a time with your careless attitude; but wake up, admire God's tenderness and patience, or evil is near. If you will not perform this duty, whoever you are, in one way or another, in one matter or another, whether spiritual or carnal wickedness, you will be tempted, you will be defiled; and where will it end? Remember Peter!

2. *Remember that you are always under the eye of Christ, the great captain of our salvation, who has told us to watch and pray that we enter not into temptation.* What do you think are the thoughts and the heart attitude of Christ when he sees a temptation hastening towards us, a storm rising about us, and we are fast asleep! Does it not grieve him to see us so exposed to danger, when he has given us warning upon warning? In the days of his flesh he considered his temptation while it was still ahead and armed himself against it. The ruler of this world was coming, he said, but he had 'nothing in me'. And shall we be negligent under his eye? Think of him coming to you as he did to Peter, when he was asleep in the garden, with

the same reproof: 'What! Could you not watch one hour?' Would it not be a grief for you to be so reproved? Or to hear him thundering from heaven against your neglect, as he did against the church of Sardis (*Rev.* 3:2)?

3. Consider that if you neglect this duty, and so fall into temptation, which you assuredly will: when you are entangled in it, *God may bring with it some heavy affliction or judgment on you which, because of your entanglement, you will be forced to look on as evidence of his anger and hatred.* And how will you bear temptation and affliction together? All your bones will be broken, and your peace and strength will be gone in a moment. This may seem but words for the present, but if it is ever your condition, you will find it to be full of woe and bitterness. Oh, then, let us strive to keep our spirits unentangled. Let us avoid all appearance of evil and all the ways leading to it. Let us particularly beware of all the courses of life, business, society, and employment that we have already found to be to our disadvantage.